RUGBY IN FOCUS

RUGBY IN FOCUS

Twenty Years of Rugby Action
Photographed by **Colin Elsey**
Written by **John Taylor**

A GRAHAM TARRANT BOOK
DAVID & CHARLES
Newton Abbot   London   North Pomfret (Vt)

(title page) *Barbarians* v *New Zealand, 1972. Sid Going tries to intercept as John Dawes passes inside to Tom David. In the background, (l to r) Ian Kirkpatrick, John Pullin, Gareth Edwards and Derek Quinnell. Moments later Edwards burst through to score his legendary try.*

British Library Cataloguing in Publication Data

Elsey, Colin
  Rugby in focus: twenty years of rugby
  action. – (A Graham Tarrant book)
  1. Rugby football – History – 20th
  century
  I. Title   II. Taylor, John   III. Series
  796.33'3'0904   GV944.85

  ISBN 0-7153-8882-7

Phototypeset by Typesetters (Birmingham) Ltd
Smethwick West Midlands
and printed in Great Britain
by Butler & Tanner   Frome and London
for David & Charles Publishers plc
Brunel House   Newton Abbot   Devon

Published in the United States of America
by David & Charles Inc
North Pomfret   Vermont 05053   USA

CONTENTS

JOHN TAYLOR
TALKING TO
COLIN ELSEY

JT Colorsport is now one of the most successful and highly respected sports photographic agencies in Britain. Was it always your ambition to set up an independent company specialising in sports photography?

CE Not really. It developed out of a sharing arrangement with my partner, Stewart Fraser, in the Sixties. We were both struggling freelancers scratching out a living from job to job, and both operating out of makeshift dark-rooms – mine was in a tiny bathroom in my flat in Hammersmith – and it seemed to make sense to share the cost. We had plenty of spare capacity, so we rented a sweatshop in Hatton Garden and went from there. Then we found ourselves covering the same events and missing out on other work, so it seemed sensible to pool pictures as well.

JT But you were always going to specialise in sport?

CE No. I studied industrial and commercial photography and Stewart was going to become an electrical engineer. But I was very keen on rugby, playing in one of the junior teams at Wasps, and I began to take some pictures while I was studying; then sold a few. When I left college it seemed natural to carry on so I sacrificed my own not too promising rugby career, settled for Sunday rugby, and decided it was better to eat.

JT How did you set about selling pictures?

CE I'd cover a match, race back to Hammersmith, and then deliver prints to various picture desks in Fleet Street in the hope that the Sunday papers would take something. Then I'd go through the same procedure on Sunday morning for the Dailies. By the time I left college I had some good contacts, so I did midweek stuff as well. But rugby was never lucrative enough by itself, so I covered athletics, golf, tennis, and anything else that came along.

JT What about equipment?

CE I cobbled it together, buying just enough film for the next job. The biggest breakthrough was buying a second-hand 400mm lens from an advertisement in *Amateur Photographer* for £80. It was the best investment I ever made because it revolutionised my work. It meant I could get right into the heart of the action for the first time.

The other big investment was motor drive. With those two things I was away, because the whole world of sports photography was being transformed. People like Gerry Cranham and the late Ed Lacey had pioneered working with 35mm reflex cameras, but a lot of firms were still using plate cameras with sheet film. For example, Sport and General had the exclusive rights to film at Twickenham and they used plate cameras, with two guys in static positions at the corner flags and one roving the touchline. There were certainly not many telephoto lenses around.

JT Was access to the big games a problem?

CE The biggest. At first I didn't even try to go to internationals, but in 1969 I just had to do something about the situation and decided to go to Cardiff on spec. I bought a ticket from a tout for the Taff end and got there early so I could get right up against the fence. The crush was dreadful because the newly installed Prince of Wales, Prince Charles, was present and there was no North Stand – the first work on the new ground was being done. In desperation I showed a policeman my Press Card and tried a feeble line about taking the wrong entrance. He knew I was lying, but took pity on me and let me over the fence, and then, as there were no bibs or armbands, gave me the nod and said, 'Go on then, you're in now, aren't you?' That bit of luck gave me the Brian Price–Noel Murphy 'knockout punch' picture.

JT Did that set the pattern?

CE Yes, but it didn't always work. A lot of the early pictures came from the terraces, but I learned to take a few hefty mates with me to clear a space. The shots of John Bevan's try against France and the sequence of Gerald Davies tackling Sillières were taken from the Taff steps in 1970, and the Centenary game at Twickenham in 1971 was from the South Terrace. But the most remarkable day was Scotland against the South Africans in 1969. I was on the bank opposite the main stand and security was extremely tight, which was the last thing I needed. There was definitely no chance of getting over the fence. They had limited the crowd and I stuck out like a sore thumb; and the light was so bad that I took only ten frames in the whole game. Then the police wanted to confiscate my film because they thought I was recording their handling of the demonstrators. But I got a perfect sequence of Ian Smith's try, which I've sold endless times since because as far as I know nobody else caught it.

Now it's much better. I was shooting colour from the start as well as black and white, which led to a contract with *Rugby World* magazine and they helped me to get into Twickenham. J. B. G. Thomas helped me in Wales, and gradually things have dropped into place.

JT What about tours?
CE 1974 was very important because I took a gamble and decided to go to South Africa, even though I hadn't the work contracted to justify it. By sleeping on floors and with a lot of help from friends, I made it work and established myself with the Press Gang. I also got some of my best-ever pictures. I was lucky because British rugby was going through a golden era.

JT How important do you think your love of the game is in your coverage?
CE It's vital. First of all you've got to want to take the pictures, and it also helps you to take the right gambles – most of the time. A knowledge of the strengths of a team gives you an in-built advantage. It works as well with individuals. When you know them, you can sometimes anticipate their next move. I can even recognise the mannerisms of some top players when they are building up for a big play.

JT Do you spend most of your time watching the game through the camera lens?
CE Yes. I'm either on the move or looking through the camera. When you are moving you are working out the technical things like light changes, and then a quick look at the position and it's back to the camera. Sometimes you get a totally false impression of a game because of it.

JT What are your biggest problems?
CE Light still governs everything. I have colour and black and white commitments and, in Britain particularly, you can often only shoot colour in the first half hour, so I must find a position that makes the most of the light available. This means I'm very often shooting from positions or angles that aren't ideal. But one has to live with the fact that rugby is a winter sport, and getting round the light problem is part of the job.

JT And do you know instantly when you have a good picture?
CE Yes. You can remember the image as you saw it through the viewfinder, and then you just pray that it is sharp. You also know when you've had a good match, and I find I respond to the big occasion just as the players do. Two of the most memorable matches for pictures were North West Counties beating the All Blacks in 1972 and the third Test in South Africa in 1974 – that was no coincidence. I knew on both occasions I had captured something special.

JT And what about failures?
CE The one that haunts me is Gareth Edwards' try for the Barbarians against the 1972 All Blacks – perhaps the most famous try ever. I had been in the perfect position at the Taff end, but the All Blacks started to dominate and I had to get my colour in the can early on, so I was making a move in their direction when Phil Bennett started to counter attack. I got two or three shots as they came past me down the touchline, and then Gareth dived right into the corner I had just left. I have been asked for that try more than any other photograph, and it still hurts when I have to admit I missed it.

LEADING FROM THE FRONT AND THE BACK

The rugby captain is a real captain. In most sports the power of the captain has been gradually eroded so that he is merely a figurehead who tosses the coin and leads the team on to the field, but in rugby he still has power.

Once the team takes the field he is in total control. There is no coach, manager or, worst of all, 'non-playing' captain to dictate the play and undermine his authority, and if the fancy takes him he can ignore all previous directives and play with five forwards and ten backs. The teams are not even allowed to leave the field at half-time so he is cocooned against interference. Some power-mad coaches have tried to circumvent this by sneaking on with the oranges, but the ruse rarely works more than once, so for eighty minutes the captain is king.

It is an awesome responsibility because rugby is one of the few games where the captain has real decisions to make. In most team sports the shape of the game would not alter if there was no captain, but in rugby, to a great extent, it is he who determines the pattern of play. The sort of rugby the team plays will be a reflection of his approach to the game.

He is consulted by the referee (and not just about the state of the light) on at least twenty occasions during a game – unless the opposition possesses those rare animals, a hooker who can throw in straight and a kick-off specialist who can propel the ball ten metres forward without hitting it directly into touch (that is, of course, the real reason for the popularity of the long kick-off). He must also make a hundred other decisions, more than one a minute. Where should the ball be thrown in a line-out? Should a penalty kick be for goal, for touch or just tapped? Should the back row attack from the base of the scrum? Will that prima donna at outside-half pass the ball if he is so instructed? If he does is it conceivable that, not having received a pass for six matches, the right wing will catch it? Only in cricket does the captain have as much influence, but he generally has much more time to ponder his next move or consult a colleague for confidence-boosting confirmation of his intended course of action.

Most rugby captains will have sympathy with Norman Gale, the Llanelli hooker, who achieved his ultimate ambition by leading Wales against the 1967 All Blacks. In the heat of the battle – hotter for us than it was for them because we were usually at full stretch to keep them out – the referee asked him if he wanted a line-out or scrum. 'Hang on,' panted Norman. 'Give us a moment, I've only just arrived.'

Not that Norman was normally indecisive. Later in the same game he decided that the recognised goal-kickers had failed once too often and elected to take a penalty kick at goal – on the 22 and right in front of the posts – himself. Anybody else would probably have rated him fifteenth choice place-kicker, but he was captain. The ball squirted forward and took off like an overloaded aeroplane, achieving a maximum height of about twelve feet between the posts. Thus Norman Gale became the only hooker ever to have kicked for Wales – a powerful man is the captain!

Norman's reign as captain did not last long, but should it have happened at all? All logic says no. Hooker has to be the worst position on the field from which to assess the state of play. Yet selectors obviously believe that hookers make good leaders. In the last Test series between the Lions and New Zealand in 1983 both captains, Ciaran Fitzgerald and Andy Dalton, were hookers. John Pullin led England to New Zealand and South Africa – beating them both – in the early Seventies; Philippe Dintrans skippered France in 1985 when Fitzgerald again fired up the Irish to take the European Championship.

The other forwards are only marginally more aware of the whole canvas, but as a unit they win the contest for captaincy over the backs hands down. A comparison of touring team captains gives the most dramatic statistics. Since the Lions began visiting New Zealand and South Africa sixteen forwards have been captain but only six backs. The only All Black back to have captained a full New Zealand side to the United Kingdom was Stu Wilson in 1983, and he was the second choice because Andy Dalton could not tour. The other eleven have been forwards.

The South African ratio is five forwards to two backs, and the Australians six to two. All of which leads to only one conclusion. Despite the importance of the captain in rugby, he is rarely selected because of his tactical awareness. The chief play maker is the outside-half, but he is one of the least popular choices. Barry John would have you believe that the only reason is that all the mundane decisions would inhibit their genius, but the fact is that only the equally mercurial Phil Bennett has captained the Lions in modern times from outside-half, and Gareth Davies, also of Wales, is the only one to have captained an International Board country in the Eighties.

My own favourite captain was undoubtedly John Dawes, the man who led Wales to the European Grand Slam in 1971, and then, later in the same year, inspired the Lions to their only Test series victory ever over the All Blacks. He was the exception to the rule, a centre threequarter who was a tactical genius and managed to bring the absolute best out of the players around him. Just by demanding an attacking philosophy, even in desperate defence, he gave everybody immense confidence and during his career he transformed the style of play of first his club, then his country, and ultimately, with great assistance from his soul-mate Carwyn James, the Lions.

New Zealand have always based their style of rugby on hard, driving forwards, so their affection for captains who lead the way by physical example is understandable. For them the back row seems to be the favourite vantage point. Brian Lochore, who has now taken over the role of coach, was a magnificent leader in the late Sixties. His method was simple – 'If I'm there I can ask the rest of you to get there too' – and he always was there. Ian Kirkpatrick and Andy Leslie followed much the same plan.

Graham Mourie broke the mould. He still led by example but demanded more from his men than the traditional All Black style. He was another captain who changed the direction of rugby in his country.

The back row has produced some notable leaders in other countries too. Mornie du Plessis of South Africa and Mervyn Davies of Wales (who might have been one of the longest serving skippers of them all had it not been for the brain haemorrhage that prematurely finished his career) followed the New Zealand school. So too, but in a very Gallic way, did Jean-Pierre Rives. He was certainly always in the thick of things but, instead of striding across the stage like a colossus, he gave a frantic impersonation of an all-in wrestling match, complete with commentary for the referee. He was even accused of cutting his head deliberately so that the famous blond mane became streaked with red and pink.

But we expect the French to have a style of their own and none was more unusual than that of Jacques Fouroux, 'Le Petit Napoleon'. One of the sights of the Seventies was to see him lacing into his forwards to get more effort from them. As a last resort he would punch and kick them, but they never once hit back, even though the player who took most punishment, Jean-Pierre Bastiat, was 6ft 7in tall while Fouroux was 5ft 3in. It was obviously an approved method because he is now the French coach.

So what does make a good captain? There is no magic formula. Some people plan, some lead by example, while some bully or cajole. It basically all comes down to respect. If you have it the team will follow you anywhere, and if you do not, nothing will persuade them that you are right.

I remember asking members of the England 'Grand Slam' pack of 1980 to put their fingers on the special qualities of Billy Beaumont. He was in a difficult position with Fran Cotton, Tony Neary and Roger Uttley, who had all done the job before, and the popular choice, Peter Wheeler, all in the team with him when he took over. It certainly was not his inspirational team talks because he found he was talking to himself as soon as a half-naked Erika Roe bounced onto the field at half-time at Twickenham – in fact, nobody could say precisely what it was that made Beaumont so exceptional, even though they all agreed he was one of the best.

Eventually Cotton got nods of approval when he ventured that, 'He was just such a good bloke, and he tried so hard that you wanted to make it all happen for him'. Being the best thinker on the game is often not enough, but being a 'good bloke' gives you at least a chance.

Willie John McBride, seen here being tackled by England's Andy Ripley at Twickenham in 1972, was a tower of strength for Ireland and the British Lions, whom he led to victory against South Africa in 1974.

Left *Former All Black captain Brian Lochore was chosen to lead the President's Overseas XV against England in 1971. In the background, Lochore's New Zealand team-mate, the legendary Colin Meads.*

John Dawes, *captain of London Welsh, Wales and the British Lions. Under his inspired leadership in 1971, the Lions beat New Zealand in a series for the first time this century.*

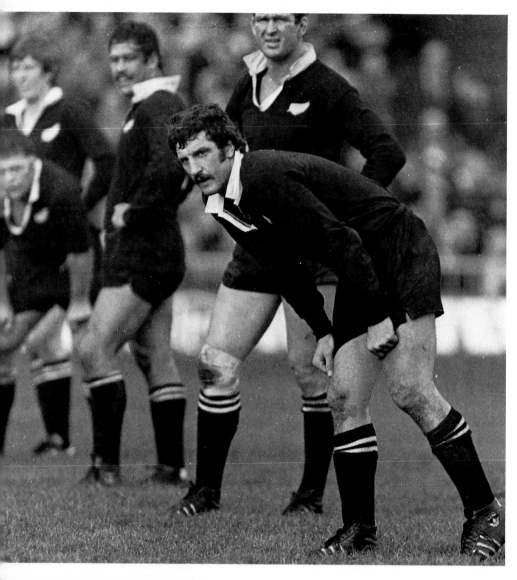

Above left *The popular Graham Mourie, who skippered the All Blacks on five European tours in five successive seasons.*

Above *Morne du Plessis leads out the Springboks to do battle with the Lions in the 2nd Test at Bloemfontein in 1980. The Springboks won 26-19.*

Above right *Andy Slack, captain of the all-conquering Wallabies in 1984, leaves Irish prop James McCoy trailing in his wake.*

Left *Jacques Fouroux – 'Le Petit Napoleon' – pint-sized captain of France, who occasionally resorted to punching and kicking his own forwards to get them on the move. Playing here against England in 1976.*

Right *Mervyn Davies scoring a try from a line-out against England in 1974. His career as captain of Wales was sadly halted by injury.*

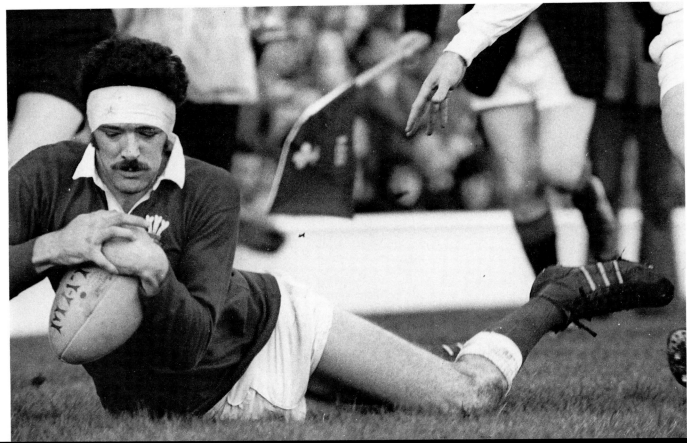

FULLBACKS

Changing the Laws is a sort of spring fever with the International Board. Most of the time it leaves scars for a couple of years and then another change causes the players the considerable frustration of relearning the old law. But just occasionally the law-makers get it right and something major is introduced that changes the game for the better, and stays with us. The last time that happened was in 1970 when what had been known as 'The Australian Dispensation' became law. It made it unprofitable to kick directly into touch from outside the 22 metre line because the line of touch would be taken from where the ball was kicked. It changed the face of the game.

The player who had to adjust most was the fullback – and it would not be an overstatement to suggest that the change of law revolutionised fullback play. The traditional role was as the totally defensive sweeper playing deep behind the back division, who fielded kicks and attempted to return them with interest if they missed touch. When that became impossible, everybody suddenly realised just how underemployed fullbacks had been.

Suddenly a new breed appeared and immediately there was a truly remarkable player to set the standard for everyone else to follow: J. P. R. Williams. Had the laws not changed he might well have been challenging me for my place as a flanker. He would surely have changed positions because his ambition to be involved in the play at every opportunity would certainly not have been satisfied by the loneliness of the long distance fullback. He did play one international as a flanker when Wales suffered bad injuries to the back row on their Australian tour in 1978. As you would expect, he made a good job of it, too.

JPR possessed a tremendous array of skills, but if you wanted to find fault it would have been with his kicking – the very thing that old-style fullbacks relied upon. Mind you, he still kicked an amazing dropped goal in the final Test in New Zealand in 1971, and a couple of vital goals in the Home Internationals.

Bob Hiller was for many people the last of the old brigade. He used the old-fashioned 'toe-end' style of place-kicking, and never polished the right toe-cap of any pair of boots he ever owned. For him goal-kicking

Bill Beaumont commiserates with rival captain Jean-Pierre Rives after England's victory over France in 1980. Beaumont led England to the 'Grand Slam' that year.

was an art. On two Lions' tours he kicked over 100 points, even though he never played in a Test and appeared in only a limited number of games, understudying first Tommy Kiernan then JPR.

Williams made his debut and a huge impact on the international scene in 1969, before the law change, so his approach to fullback play was very much his own. The only other player to make the transition easily was Pierre Villepreux of France. He played from 1967–72 when the French were playing a much more fluent running style of rugby than the Home Countries (what's new?) so an attacking fullback, especially one with the speed of Villepreux, was a natural choice.

There were now far more qualities to be considered when choosing a fullback, and it became one of the glamour positions on the field. Far more young players decided to give it a try instead of opting for outside-half or centre. Within two years Scotland produced their own version of the new breed. Andy Irvine played for Scotland for a decade and holds the world record for the number of points scored in major internationals, with 301, if you count Romania, and 289 if you do not. Unlike Williams, he was a superb goal-kicker but as Lee Trevino once said, talking about his own lack of length, 'God never gives everything to one man.' Irvine's weakness was his defensive play.

Nevertheless, he was a superb attacking fullback and had the pace to play on the wing when necessary. Scotland used him there four times and, with Williams the first choice fullback, he also played two Tests for the 1974 Lions in South Africa on the wing.

Another fullback to span a decade in international football was Dusty Hare. He too has forged his reputation around his goal-kicking, but there is much more to him as a player than that. He holds the English points record with 240. He also holds the world record for the number of points scored in first-class rugby, with a tally in the region of 6,000.

The outstanding player of the Eighties so far has been the Frenchman, Serge Blanco. His loose-limbed athleticism allows him to join the line from incredibly deep positions and unexpected angles, and his sleight of hand is worthy of a basketball player. 'For me to kick is defeat – it is my very final option,' is his motto.

Roger Gould of Australia is a big man who takes on some of the goal-kicking duties, but his main contribution to the outstanding 1984 Wallabies was as an attacker. The great Don Clarke, he of the siege-gun boot and sixteen-stone frame, would now almost certainly be forced into the forwards because even the New Zealanders are going for smaller, slighter men who can run the ball. There was much shaking of heads from the old-stagers when Alan Hewson was carried off suffering from exposure while playing for Wellington in 1983, and still more when he appeared in thermal undershirt and fingerless mittens against the Lions in Dunedin.

J. P. R. Williams won a record fifty-five caps for Wales in an international career which began in 1969 and ended in 1981. His fearless catching and tackling, his powerful running and fiercely competitive spirit made him supreme as an attacking fullback. Above JPR about to be tackled by Alastair Cranston after a typically determined charge past Andy Irvine. Steve Fenwick is in support. Wales v Scotland, 1976.

JPR, covered in blood, back in action for Bridgend after the notorious raking incident in which the Welsh fullback had fallen foul of All Black John Ashworth's boot. Williams came back onto the field with several stitches in his face, but still managed to give the New Zealanders, among them Graham Mourie and Mark Taylor left, a run for their money.

England's Bob Hiller playing against Ireland in 1972. He used the old-fashioned 'toe-end' style of place-kicking to notably good effect.

Concentration . . . suspense . . . delight. Dusty Hare kicks another penalty, and England are on the way to an historic 15-9 victory over the All Blacks at Twickenham in 1983.

Andy Irvine shows his customary speed and flair in attack to score a brilliant solo try for the Lions against a Combined XV in 1977. Tony Neary and Bill Beaumont watch him go.

Playing against the Lions at Dunedin in 1983, Alan Hewson sets a new fashion for New Zealand fullbacks with his thermal undershirt and fingerless mittens.

For thirteen years, Tom Kiernan's immaculate goal-kicking technique did Ireland proud. In all, he won fifty-four caps for his country, a record twenty-four of them as captain.

The acceleration and agility of Frenchman Serge Blanco has made him the most exciting fullback in the game today. Here he sets up team-mate Didier Codorniou in the match against Scotland in 1985.

Below *Australia's Roger Gould, another attacking fullback who likes to run with the ball.*

Below right *Pierre Villepreux turned in some outstanding performances for France in the late Sixties and early Seventies. This one against England in 1971.*

Over *The unmistakable figure of J. P. R. Williams taking on the Scots at Cardiff Arms Park in 1976.*

THE LIONS
IN NEW ZEALAND

Noel Coward is reputed to have summed up New Zealand by saying he once made a visit but arrived on a Sunday and found it closed, so he went away again. If he had made another visit during a Lions' tour, he would have left with a completely different impression.

The whole country comes to life and there is only one subject under discussion – Rugby. New Zealand may be a funny little Do-It-Yourself country on the other side of the world which reminds many people of Britain in the Fifties, but it provides the ultimate rugby examination. The Lions have been touring there for over 100 years, but only the 1971 team came away with a series victory.

After three weeks of eating, talking and sleeping rugby in 1983, John Carleton, the England wing, declared that he now knew what it must be like to live in Wales. It is a difficult country to tour. Every match is hard because the opposing forwards are always strong and physical, even if they are not very skilful, and the generosity and hospitality is often overwhelming. Several Lions' teams have simply worn themselves out. Boredom is another big factor which can undermine a team. Changing towns twice a week for three months is not something that everybody can cope with, especially when one town is much the same as the one before, with the same round of civic receptions, rugby club functions and visits to local schools.

The 1977 Lions had another thing working against them, the weather. They happened to encounter the worst winter New Zealand had seen for a very long time. It rained wherever they went. On his return home the captain, Phil Bennett, said he was going to write a guide to New Zealand snooker halls, as they were the only bits of scenery he ever saw.

John Dawes, who had captained the 1971 Lions, went back this time as coach. It was not a happy experience. After the success of the 1971 team, and the 1974 team in South Africa, people expected the Lions to win and when they began badly, there was heavy criticism levelled at the coach and the players. Dawes reacted by defending his players and refusing the press

access to them. The whole party became very insular and kept themselves apart, which made life 12,000 miles away from home even more lonely. Nevertheless, they still went very close to sharing the series. Having lost the first Test, they levelled the series at Christchurch. The All Blacks went ahead again with a decisive victory at Dunedin in the third Test, which should have left the last Test a formality, with an unhappy team thinking more of returning home than drawing the series. Only the 1959 Lions had ever won the final Test.

The 1977 team almost emulated them. With just minutes to go they were leading 9-6, but then fatally missed a kick to touch and Laurie Knight squeezed over in the right-hand corner to give the All Blacks victory 10-9.

Willie John McBride, captain of the 1974 Lions and a veteran of five tours as a player, was chosen as manager of the 1983 Lions. This was a new kind of tour with only eighteen matches instead of the customary twenty-four or more. The idea was to ease the pressure on the players by shortening the time they were away. All it did was to make life even tougher in New Zealand, and Willie John was desperately unhappy with the new format.

He accused the New Zealand Rugby Union of thinking only of the revenue the tour was earning, because they simply dropped all the weakest fixtures and moved some of the toughest games to midweek. There was also just a two-week gap between all the Tests, which meant that there was no chance to experiment. As it turned out, it would have made no difference. Andy Dalton's forwards were much too strong for the British pack, especially after Bob Norster was ruled out through injury, and for the first time since 1966 the Lions lost all four Tests. McBride wrote a damning report about the length of the tour, demanding that there should be at least twenty-two matches or that the number of Tests be reduced to three. The International Board decided on the latter. However, even that may not be satisfactory – because at the same time they reduced the total number of matches to thirteen.

The pitch for the Lions' match against the New Zealand Juniors at Wellington in 1977 was such a quagmire that at times the sport appeared more like wrestling in mud than rugby. Above *Moss Keane's mouthwash at halftime looks startlingly like ectoplasm.* Right *a mud-caked Fran Cotton takes on a distinctly primeval look.*

Phil Bennett, accompanied by the Lions' mascot, leads out the side for the 2nd Test at Christchurch in 1977. Tane Norton does the honours for New Zealand.

Above right *According to North Auckland's ferocious-looking mascot, on a pre-match parade at Whangarei in 1977, the Lions are about to be chewed up. In the event, the home side was beaten 18-7.*

Right *No hard feelings. Terry Cobner and Bill Osborne shake hands in the traditional spirit of the game after New Zealand's victory in the 3rd Test at Dunedin in 1977. The score was 19–7.*

1

2

3

4

5

6

The Lions' captain Phil Bennett displays superb acceleration and body swerve as he weaves his way through the Auckland defence to score a dazzling individual try. The match resulted in a crushing victory for the Lions, 34-15.

Winger John Carleton leads the way with forwards Paxton, O'Driscoll and Winterbottom in support. 4th Test, 1983.

Jock Hobbs wins possession of the ball to feed Dave Loveridge. Bob Norster and Maurice Colclough are left standing. 2nd Test, 1983.

Left *Dave Loveridge on the receiving end again, this time from Gary Whetton. Ciaran Fitzgerald arrives on the scene too late.*

Above right *All Black forwards Tane Norton and Bill Bush get the better of Bill Beaumont and Peter Brown, while scrum-half Lyn Davis gets the ball. 3rd Test, 1977.*

An historic moment in the 3rd Test. Forced on to the defensive by the powerful Lions' pack, New Zealand resorts to the unprecedented tactic of a three-man scrum – and wins the ball for Lyn Davis.

*Lions' prop Graham Price attempts to
charge down Sid Going's clearing kick in
the 2nd Test, 1977.*

*In the 3rd Test at Dunedin in 1977, New
Zealand score a try with almost the first
move of the match. Centre Bruce
Robertson cuts through the defence, kicks
past fullback Andy Irvine, and scorer Ian
Kirkpatrick is first to the loose ball.*

3rd Test at Dunedin in 1983:

Left *No 8 Murray Mexted and Andy Haden catch the Lions in possession. Flanker Jim Calder tries to make sure the All Blacks don't get away with it.*

Below left *Graham Price puts all his weight into tackling Dave Loveridge. Round and about: Andy Dalton, Ciaran Fitzgerald, Maurice Colclough and John Ashworth.*

Right *A moment to savour for try-scorer John Rutherford.*

Opposing captains Andy Dalton and Ciaran Fitzgerald exchange shirts after New Zealand's series-clinching victory.

LIFE ON TOUR

With training almost every day and matches twice a week, official functions to attend and constant travelling, life on tour for the players and the rest of the party can be very demanding. Some relaxation therefore is essential – whatever form it takes.

*Ian McGeechan and Andy Irvine
surrounded by admiring supporters in
Fiji, 1977.*

*Waiting around airport lounges is an
inevitable part of any tour these days.
Here, on the 1980 tour of South Africa,
duty boy for the day Derek Quinnell has
the additional responsibility of seeing that
no harm comes to the Lions' mascot.*

*Assistant manager Noel Murphy heads a
parade of vintage vehicles carrying the
Lions into Pretoria, 1980.*

Dusty Hare, who is no mean cricketer, despite the outfit, goes into bat at Waitangi, 1983.

Right *Bobby Windsor training with the Lions at Westport, New Zealand, 1977.*

Below right *The 1977 Lions don't appear to be too disturbed by their confrontation with a Maori warrior.*

Ollie Campbell, more professionally turned out, shows impressive form for the Lions against South African Players and Press, 1980.

Steve Boyle hits heartily to leg, with a padless Roger Baird behind the stumps and Jim Calder in the gully. Waitangi, 1983.

Nigel Melville lines up a putt with the assistance of Roger Baird. Waitangi, 1983.

Opposite Peter Whiting, supported by his captain Ian Kirkpatrick, wins the line-out from Mervyn Davies and Dai Morris. Wales v New Zealand, 1972.

Four of the 1977 Lions find time to relax in Fiji after their bruising tour of New Zealand: (l to r) Gordon Brown, Doug Morgan, Phil Orr, Steve Fenwick.

Winger *Stu Wilson rounding Roger Baird in the 4th Test against the Lions in 1983 to score his 17th try for New Zealand – an all-time record for his country.*

The Argentinian fly-half Hugo Porta playing for the South African Barbarians against the Junior Springboks in 1980.

Opposite *Graham Price of Pontypool, Wales and the British Isles.*

Roger Spurrell of Bath holding aloft the John Player Cup after beating London Welsh in the 1985 final. They were to win again in 1986, making it three in a row.

Gareth Evans and Allan Martin tempt fate with their impression of two Maori gods – which may have had something to do with the Lions losing the series 3-1.

Opposite *The magical Mark Ella on his way to a try against Scotland during the Australians' 'Grand Slam' tour of 1984. With this, Ella became the only player to have scored a try against each of the four Home Countries in the same international series.*

Mike Roberts, aided and abetted by Glyn Shaw, in a line-out duel with Willie John McBride. Wales v Ireland, 1973.

Nothing too highbrow for J. P. R. Williams as he soaks up the sunshine in Johannesburg in 1974.

Gone fishing – Alan Tomes in Durban, 1980.

Right *About to take a dive in the Bay of Islands: l to r Peter Winterbottom, Bob Norster, John Carleton, Maurice Colclough, Trevor Ringland, 'Staff' Jones. Lions' tour of New Zealand, 1983.*

Below right *Maurice Colclough dressed to kill.*

Far right *Willie John McBride with a big one – Sardinia Bay, Port Elizabeth, 1974.*

Andy Ripley demonstrates his prowess on the surfboard. South Africa, 1974.

Lions' coach John Dawes at Christchurch in 1977, watched by a discerning audience of aspiring All Blacks.

Above left *Not the thigh bones of ancient Springbok forwards, but the remains of some of the inmates at the Addo Elephant Park at Port Elizabeth. Phil Blakeway, Nick Youngs and game warden, on the 1984 England tour of South Africa.*

Left *Andy Irvine, always popular with the ladies, at Westport, New Zealand, in 1977.*

Homeward bound. The 1977 Lions depart New Zealand, stopping off briefly in Fiji before returning to the UK.

SNAP SELECTION 1

Far left *Cpt G. C. Campbell and a young John Taylor playing in the Surrey v The Army game in 1967. When the photograph first appeared in* The Times, *Colin Elsey managed to get both names wrong in the caption. Now, twenty years on, he is happy to put the record straight.*

Left *Maurice Colclough getting up a head of steam for Rosslyn Park against Richmond in 1979.*

Below left *A close encounter for Derek Quinnell, Terry Cobner, Allan Martin and Frenchman Francis Haget. Wales v France, 1978.*

Ian Jones of London Welsh having a hard time of it against Newbridge in 1972.

Andy Ripley leads Chris Ralston, John Watkins, Steve Smith and Alan Old (behind) in an England charge against Australia in 1973.

ON THE WING

I tried playing on the wing for half a season at school. The experiment finished when one cold and almost frosty morning I waited fifty-nine minutes for contact with the ball (we only played thirty minutes each way in the Under 13s) and then got it in the parts that hurts even little boys most, via the boot of my opposite number. It was not malicious. He let fly from five yards because he did not relish the thought of being tackled. Not having touched the ball himself before in the game, he was also frozen stiff. If only he had told me – I had no intention of getting in his way.

Life is not very different in the first-class game (except that seniors are probably wise to the surprise kick). In one recent international, played in fine weather, England's Rory Underwood had the ball in his hands for nine seconds and was involved in play for a total of less than thirty, yet he was the fastest and most elusive runner on his team. Still, he must be used to it. Surveys have shown that wingers run less than any other players – forwards tend to run twice as far as backs – and stand idle for the longest periods, even though they are invariably the best athletes.

At one time wingers were allowed to throw in to line-outs to keep themselves interested, but even that perk has been taken away from them by the greedy hookers. No wonder they so often make a hash of their one big opportunity. They are bored to death. In most teams the winger spends most of his time with his fingers crossed, hoping that the ball will reach him as it goes through the hands of half-backs, centres and probably the fullback too. It explains why so many passes are dropped by wingers – they have forgotten to uncross their fingers.

With so many crosses to bear it's perhaps not surprising that wingers are often the most aggressive characters in a team. They spend so much time building themselves up for nothing, and suffer so much general frustration, that they sometimes explode with fury when they do get into the action. Maurice Richards of Wales, the only player since the war to score four tries in a Five Nations Championship game – he turned England inside out in 1969 – was a typical case. Off the field he was the mildest, gentlest teetotal Baptist lay preacher you could ever wish to meet, the antithesis of the popular conception of an archetypal rugby man. But on the field he became a screaming dervish, cursing referee and opponents in equal measure if they frustrated his ambitions. Mind you, they seldom succeeded. He was a devastating runner

and the only pity was that the Welsh fans saw so little of him before he turned professional.

More recently most of the fire and brimstone merchants have come from New Zealand. Prickliest of all was Grant Batty. He might have been small, but he was quite prepared to take on the world and exuded hate for the eighty minutes he was on the field like nobody else I have ever seen. Bernie Fraser and Stu Wilson also changed character completely the moment they pulled on an All Black jersey. Belligerence Incorporated would have been a better name for them than Ebony and Ivory.

The exception was Bryan Williams, who holds the record number of caps for a New Zealand winger with thirty-six, plus two more as a centre. Williams might have looked ferocious when he was running, but he was really a gentle giant as ready with a smile on the field as off it.

So what makes a good winger? The only absolute prerequisite is speed – given that the methods of beating a man are as varied as the shapes of the players. At one end of the scale there is Gerald Davies, as neat and nimble as Nijinsky, and at the other another great Welsh wing – John Bevan – who was quickly grabbed for Rugby League. Bevan preferred the shortest route between two points even if there were people in the way. New Zealanders became great admirers of his 'Maori side-step' after the infamous Lions match against Canterbury when he exploded straight through Fergie McCormick and two of the back row to score a remarkable try. To suggest that Bevan could not beat a man is to do him a great disservice, but one did feel he derived greater satisfaction from blasting straight through people.

In between the two ends of the winger spectrum there is an infinite number of variables. David Duckham weighed in at over fourteen stones but was a good combination of the two. There were few finer sights than Duckham in full flight, but he could also beat a man with an outside swerve or a heavily telegraphed but hard-to-stop jink inside. Bryan Williams employed the same sort of technique.

All the wings featured here were or are world class players, but one stands out above the rest: Gerald Davies. I was lucky enough to play alongside him at college, club and national level for over ten years – we were briefly the centre pairing at Loughborough – and his genius for the game never stopped surprising me.

Perhaps the picture of wingers as petulant prima donnas just waiting to parade their pedigrees is overpainted, and perhaps the scarcity of ball is overstated because most of the individual try-scoring records are held by wings. But they are undoubtedly a breed unto themselves. However, please don't think I don't respect them – I just wish I'd been enough of a thoroughbred to join them. Some of the greatest memories in the game are of the great wings in full flight.

The speedy Mike Slemen handing off Elgan Rees. Wales v England, 1979.

London Counties' Alan Richards is left with a familiar view of Grant Batty as the All Black winger scores a try against them in 1972.

Gerald Davies was one of the greatest wing threequarters of all time. His remarkable acceleration, pace, side-step and swerve constantly created havoc among the opposition. He went with the British Lions to South Africa and New Zealand, and made forty-six appearances for Wales, sharing with Gareth Edwards the record number of tries scored by a Welshman – twenty – in internationals. Apart from the tries he scored himself, he made countless more for others to score.

Left Davies on his way to a try against England in 1971.

Davies is caught by Ireland's Arthur McMaster and Tony Ensor . . . but still manages to make the ball available to Gareth Edwards . . . who passes Stewart McKinney to score a try. Wales v Ireland, 1973.

David Campese, prolific try-scorer for Australia, leaves England's Nick Stringer behind, with Simon Poidevin and Mark Ella in support. Twickenham, 1984.

Above right *Patrick Estève takes off to score a spectacular try against England in 1984, with Barley and Underwood coming second and third.*

Right *The great All Black winger Bryan Williams thunders past a swooping Fergus Slattery in the 1974 Barbarians game. Williams holds the record number of caps for a New Zealand winger.*

Elgan Rees and J. P. R. Williams close in on the Maori winger Bernie Fraser, whose devastating partnership with fellow All Black Stu Wilson earned them the nickname 'Ebony and Ivory'.

David Duckham, England's most-capped back, was a dazzling combination of power, agility and speed, equally at home in the centre as he was on the wing. *Above* He fends off Dick Milliken in the match against Ireland in 1974. *Right* A race to the ball with another outstanding winger, France's Jean-François Gourdon.

Above left The powerfully-built Welshman John Bevan believed in taking the shortest route between two points, even if there were others in the way. Here playing for the Barbarians against E. Midlands in 1973.

Left Laurie Monaghan's tackle comes too late to prevent winger J. J. Williams scoring the third try in Wales' 28-3 victory over Australia in 1975.

Over John Carleton outstrips Welsh defenders Clive Rees and the diving Gwyn Evans to score at Twickenham in 1982.

Stu Wilson aquaplanes across the line to equal Ian Kirkpatrick's individual try-scoring record for New Zealand. 3rd Test v British Lions, 1983.

Rory Underwood, whose lightning acceleration makes him the most exciting English winger of recent years, in a predatory mood against Australia in 1984.

Brendan Moon opens the Australian account against Midland Counties in 1981 with the first try of the tour.

Welsh winger Maurice Richards brushes aside Ireland's Alan Duggan at Cardiff in 1969. Later the same year, he was to score a record four tries in the match against England.

SPOT OF BOTHER

'Get your retaliation in first,' was the advice of the late Carwyn James, coach extraordinaire, after a disgraceful display of thuggery from the Canterbury forwards had almost wrecked the 1971 Lions' tour the week before the first Test. It has been much quoted ever since, but most people misunderstood the remark. In his subtle way, Carwyn was telling us that while he did not condone violence, he did not expect us to sit back and soak it up. It was typical of the difficulty that rugby has in dealing with the whole subject. If you ask the people in the game, nobody supports gratuitous violence, but they all accept that it goes on and are generally unwilling to do anything about it.

Willie John McBride took Carwyn's dictum a stage further in South Africa in 1974, with the '99' call. If any individual became involved in any trouble, the call would go out and the whole pack would wade in. He was determined to show the opposition that his men would not be intimidated; but since then, mass brawling – which often looks far worse than it is – has become more frequent in rugby. Some top officials, like George Crawford, the English referee who walked off the field and left the Bristol and Newport players to their fight, believe that some teams have developed the ploy to confuse the referee and make it impossible for him to single out the real troublemakers.

In recent years there has been a greater determination on the part of administrators to stamp out dirty play. First England and then Wales slapped a ban on players being selected for the national team if they had been sent off in the same season. That determination has not been matched by the clubs. There is still a hard core of players and coaches and club officials who not only condone it, but believe that it is all part of the game. They secretly admire the thugs whose philosophy is that if you cannot win by fair means you resort to foul.

Fortunately, at the very top level, there are now three referees on the field, which makes it much more difficult for the player who insists on a sly dig on the blind-side, as England's Steve Brain found to his cost in the 1986 Championship. England began with a cracking try against Ireland, only to be called back because of his punch after the ball had gone.

Referees are also now much more willing to send off players than they were twenty years ago, and players themselves are prepared to resort to the courts if they are the victims of assault. All this means that, contrary to some opinion, the game is in fact much cleaner than it was back in the Sixties.

Every time a rugby player takes the field he risks serious injury, even if the game is played totally within the laws, so there is no room for psychopaths; but it is impossible to expect players to be perfectly behaved all the time. In a fiercely combative contact sport there will always be spontaneous combustion, and it is important that disciplinary committees differentiate between that and the premeditated act of violence. Wales now recognise that the offence for which a player has been sent off should be taken into account when dishing out suspensions. A punch means an automatic four-week ban for a first offender, while a kick carries a minimum of six weeks. It seems sensible. There is a wealth of difference between two men standing toe to toe, having lost their tempers – stupid but hardly criminal – and the thug who is quite prepared to kick a player lying on the ground.

Having delivered the lecture, I must admit that some of the thugs had style. One second row in the late Sixties would regularly slip his binding at the first scrum and lean through to tickle the chin of the opposing hooker, just to let him know what was possible if there were any problems. The second time he did it for real, but was not always accurate. I saw several of his own props with black eyes.

There are a great number of wrong targets being singled out, and mistaken identity. I remember the Welsh hooker Brian Rees taking a right-hander and demanding to know what it was for. 'Biting' said his opponent, showing a full set of teeth marks, at which point Brian grinned broadly to reveal a huge toothless gap. On that occasion his opposite number had the modesty to apologise.

Sometimes it is the referee who gets it wrong. Phil O'Callaghan, the Irish prop, was once ordered from the field when all the players knew he was not the man who had stamped on an opponent in a ruck. They tried to persuade the referee, but it soon became obvious that he was not going to change his mind. O'Callaghan resigned himself to making the lonely walk, but in a last gesture of frustration demanded to know who he had offended against. When the man was pointed out, he rushed over and kicked him on the backside, then turned to the referee and yelled, 'I'm not going off for doing nothing', and then headed for the touchline.

Generally rugby players do not make mountains out of molehills when it comes to foul-play or injury, but there was one notorious exception: the incident in which Brian Price felled Noel Murphy in front of the Prince of Wales at Cardiff Arms Park in 1969. I am not condoning the act (although Murphy had dished out a great deal throughout the match), but just look at the photograph. Have you ever seen anybody who is knocked unconscious manage to cradle his head in his hands first. As they would say in New Zealand, 'Pure Hollywood'.

Welsh forward Brian Price floors Ireland's Noel Murphy with a perfect right cross to the side of the head at Cardiff in 1969. Among those who saw the punch thrown was Prince Charles, making his first public appearance as the Prince of Wales.

Mike Burton has the unenviable reputation of having been sent off in both hemispheres. Above *The clock shows that the match is only a few minutes old as he gets his marching orders, when playing for England against Australia in the 2nd Test at Brisbane in 1975.* Left *An ironic bow to the crowd and the England selectors who were there as he prematurely departs the Gloucestershire v Hertfordshire match in 1975. The sending-off cost Burton at least one England cap.*

Referee David Burnett points to the touchline and Welsh flanker Paul Ringer is sent off early in the game against England in 1980. Between them, holding his jaw, is the injured party, John Horton.

Violence flares in the 2nd Test against the Lions in 1977, as All Black prop Bill Bush uses boot and fist on the fallen Graham Price.

Above left *Not so civil behaviour by The Army in one of their mid-Sixties games against the Civil Service.*

Left *Scotland's Doug Morgan on the receiving end of a punch from 'Stack' Stevens, the England prop, in 1973. Gordon Strachan, Nairn MacEwan and Gordon Brown display suitable consternation.*

Winger John Carleton is in obvious agony as he receives treatment for the leg injury – the result of a particularly violent tackle from Bernie Fraser – which put him out of the England v New Zealand game in 1983.

1

2

3

4

A great try, but the end of the tour for the Lions' winger Peter Squires. The expression on his face as he nears the line clearly shows the moment when his hamstring fails him. Squires returned to the field after treatment, but played in no further games. The match, against NZ Maoris, ended in a narrow victory for the 1977 Lions, 22-19.

England No 8 John Scott gets an uncomfortably close view of the boot of his long-standing rival Jean-Luc Joinel at Paris in 1982.

5

IN THE CENTRE

Centres used to be the glamour boys of the game. As a child in the Fifties, it was always Bleddyn Williams and Jack Matthews of Wales, then Jeff Butterfield and Phil Davies of England, who I wanted to emulate. Now those days have gone and the centres have a totally different role. We rarely see the dashing outside break which carves a great hole through the midfield, followed by an imperious dummy or a pass that gives a try on a plate to the wing.

Theoretically, it should be easier now because there is more room. Wing forwards are no longer allowed to follow the ball at a scrummage, they must remain bound until it emerges from the back row; and at line-outs, the backs are now forced to remain twenty metres apart until the ball is released. But it has not worked out that way. Patterns of defence have totally changed. The back row no longer commits itself to going for the half-backs, and at least one man is usually in position to try to pick off the centre who makes a break. So, the centres have become the playmakers from the set pieces and have to wait for the second phase, when the defence has been drawn out of position, before they find room to go themselves.

In attack, passing has become the all-important skill. The player who can take and give a pass accurately, all in one stride, will create more space than the greatest acceleration in the world. The king of the passers over the last twenty years has been John Dawes. His presence was not always the most obtrusive, but it was no coincidence that London Welsh, Wales and the 1971 British Lions were the most exciting movers of the ball when he was playing. Since then only the Australians, on their 1984 tour to the UK and Ireland, have matched the speed of movement and the fluency that he produced.

Unkind contemporaries are allowed to suggest that it was a skill born of expediency. He was a flanker at school and while a number of failed centres, like me, were forced to move into the pack, he moved the other way – and will sometimes admit that he was never the fastest back in the West. Having said that, he always found an extra yard when a flyer was trying to get past him.

Tackling is the other skill that a centre must positively enjoy, because he will be required to make tackles from every possible angle and any weakness will soon be exposed. David Duckham, who is still the most-capped back for England, having played twenty-two times on the wing and fourteen times in the

centre, always claimed that it was the most difficult part of switching between the two positions. He found it easy to tackle on the wing after playing at centre, but then found it very difficult when asked to revert. That is one of the reasons why there is very little interchange between the two positions. Duckham and Gerald Davies both made the switch from centre to wing to make the most of their remarkable running talents – which supports the theory that there is now less room in midfield – but I cannot think of one player who has successfully moved the other way.

In the modern game, there is perhaps more in common between the outside-half and the centres. Some would even argue that there is more of a partnership between outside-half and inside-centre than there is between the centres themselves. The Antipodean countries acknowledge this by referring to them as first and second five-eighth.

There are very few players who can switch back and fore, but one spectacular example was Mike Gibson. He is the world's most-capped player with a total of eighty-one internationals in a career that spanned fifteen years. Of his sixty-nine Irish caps, forty were at centre, twenty-five at fly-half and four on the wing. For the Lions, he played four Tests in 1966 at centre, four Tests in 1968 at fly-half, and four more in 1971 as a centre, with Barry John inside him when both had been selected for the tour as halves. Gibson took it all in his stride – but then he was one of the most complete players the world has ever seen. It has often been said that a settled centre partnership is the key to a successful back division, but there have been very few at international level in the recent past.

You cannot think of Duckham without thinking of John Spencer; the New Zealand pairing of Bruce Robertson and Bill Osborne had a great understanding; Clive Woodward and Paul Dodge worked well together; and Steve Fenwick alongside Ray Gravell made a few good players go weak at the knees – but, in general, centres have had to learn to adapt to new partners very frequently. The longest partnership must be that between Jim Renwick and Ian McGeechan. They played together twenty-six times, with Renwick winning fifty caps in all (to share the Scottish record with Sandy Carmichael) and McGeechan thirty-two. Remarkably, in all that time, McGeechan did not score one try – proof that the centre's role is now more that of try-maker than try-scorer.

Centres come in all shapes and sizes. They vary their game to suit their own particular strengths, but very few have their philosophy worked out as well as Arthur Lewis, the crash-tackling, hard-running Welsh centre from Ebbw Vale. 'Centre play is simple,' he used to say. 'If they do have the ball I do knock 'em down as hard as I can, and if I have the ball I still do knock 'em down.' Most people would settle for a player like that.

Clive Woodward, perhaps the most elusive of modern English centres, leaves Norrie Rowan and Jim Aitken behind as he executes the perfect dummy on his way to a try against Scotland in 1981.

Lions' captain and coach John Dawes, a tough, thrusting, versatile centre, and a brilliant tactician. Playing here against Ireland in 1977.

Ireland's Michael Kiernan on the run against Australia in 1984.

England centre John Spencer clearly thinks he can handle John Dawes with his eyes closed, at Cardiff in 1971.

Roland Bertranne, one in a long line of outstanding French centres and the most-capped player for his country, is tackled by Ken Plummer (obscured by Jean-Pierre Bastiat) against England in 1976. Mike Slemen is on the left.

Ireland's Mike Gibson was one of the most complete players the game has ever seen, as much at home on the wing or at fly-half as he was in the centre. Here he miraculously forces his way past the formidable Welsh quartet of Jeff Young, Gareth Edwards, Mervyn Davies and J. P. R. Williams to score at Cardiff in 1973.

Opposite *The 1977 All Blacks issue a warning to the French at Parc des Princes with the traditional haka.*

Two South African stars in action for the Overseas Unions against the Five Nations in 1986: centre Danie Gerber, passing the ball, watched by fly-half Naas Botha. England's Rory Underwood (left) is in pursuit with Frenchman Philippe Sella racing back in defence.

Photocall for Dusty Hare and friends at the former England fullback's Nottinghamshire farm.

Left *The charismatic French captain Jean-Pierre Rives in action at Twickenham.*

Classically controlled back-row play from No 8 Mervyn Davies as flanker Jan Ellis closes in. 3rd Test, South Africa v British Lions, 1974.

Hika Reid gets a facial mudpack playing for New Zealand against the US Eagles at the 1983 Hong Kong Sevens.

Right *A dislocated finger for Welsh fly-half Malcolm Dacey. Both finger and player were immediately pressed back into service.*

All Black scrum-half Sid Going in the clutches of Dai Morris and Mervyn Davies, with Ian Kirkpatrick coming to the rescue. Wales v New Zealand, 1972.

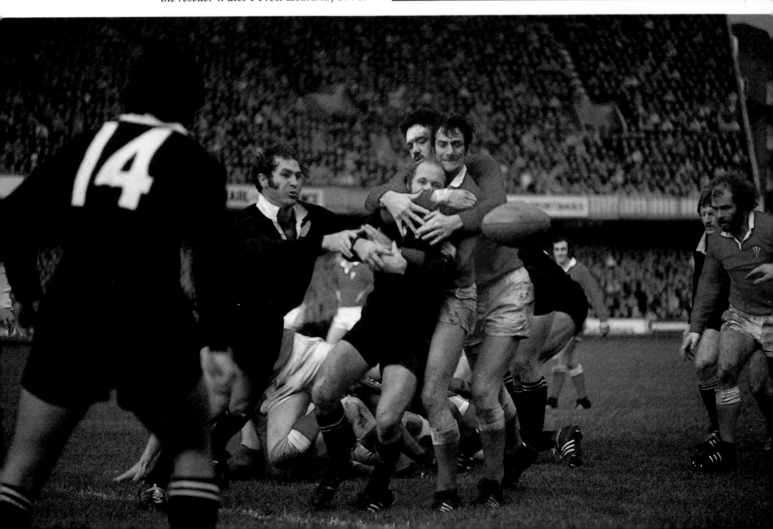

Welshman Steve Fenwick, never an easy man to stop, in typically aggressive mood for the Lions against Auckland in 1977.

Opposite *Victor and vanquished:* opposing captains Andy Dalton and Ciaran Fitzgerald acknowledge the crowd after the final Test in Auckland in 1983.

The perfect end to a successful tour. Australian skipper Andy Slack is carried in triumph from the field by Simon Poidevin and Steve Williams after the Barbarians game in 1984.

England's Peter Preece does his best to hang onto Welsh centre Arthur Lewis at Cardiff in 1973.

Ian McGeechan, who astonishingly failed to score a try in thirty-two appearances for Scotland, skilfully combines side-step with split-second change of direction to carve a hole in the North Auckland defence and cross the line for the British Lions in 1977.

Ray Gravell, whose partnership with Steve Fenwick was the driving force of Welsh back-play in the late Seventies, bursts through a tackle by Colin Deans to score a try against Scotland in 1978.

Paul Dodge making a solo break against Wales at Twickenham in 1982.

Right *Bruce Robertson is one of the few centres of genuine world class to have emerged from New Zealand since the war. With him in the picture is another, Bill Osborne, who played alongside Robertson in many internationals.*

Above left *Hugo MacNeill misses with the final kick of the game to leave the 1983 Lions trailing Canterbury 22-20.*

Above *Fullback Alastair Hignell fails to level the score against Wales in 1978, and England lose 9-6.*

Brian McKechnie's penalty, following a controversial line-out decision right at the end of the game against Wales in 1978, saw New Zealand victors by 13-12.

SNAP SELECTION 2

An ecstatic Dusty Hare lands the second of his three penalties, which capped two Welsh tries to give England's 1980 'Grand Slam' side victory, 9-8.

The scoreboard tells the story at Cardiff in 1972. Stewards are about to change the figure 16 on the board in anticipation of Phil Bennett's last-minute kick going over. In the event, the kick was wide of the mark and the score remained 19-16 in favour of New Zealand.

FIJIAN INTERLUDE

A rugby match in Suva, where there is enthusiastic support for the game at all levels. The home side, Nadroga, take advantage of the balmy weather to change outdoors, and at the end of a hotly-contested game the two teams line up to shake hands in traditional Fijian style. The post-match discussion is a family affair.

GRAND SLAM WALLABIES

When Alan Jones, the coach to the 1984 Australian team, spoke confidently of winning the Grand Slam over the four home countries at the first press conference of the tour, he was dismissed as a loud mouth and excused because people knew he used to write political speeches. Two months later he had made his boast come true, and had given rugby the biggest shot in the arm since the 1971 Lions beat New Zealand.

There was no reason to believe him. Australia had always proved difficult to beat on home ground, but had never managed to produce the same sort of form on the wetter, heavier grounds of Europe; but this was a very different sort of Australian team. Jones was outspoken to the point of arrogance about the shortcomings in world rugby. He criticised the shortage of skilled coaching and declared that British players lacked confidence on the ball. His own players, he said, were happy with the ball in their hands and would surprise the British players with their speed and distribution. An early defeat by Cardiff sent the disbelievers home chuckling with glee, but a convincing win over England soon wiped the smiles off their faces.

A week later Ireland were also beaten and it was obvious that while the touring party lacked depth, it had a very good Test fifteen.

Wales were expected to put them in their place, but instead the Australian forwards destroyed them, scoring four tries – including a pushover – in their 28-9 victory. Now it was left to Scotland, winners of the Grand Slam the previous season, but they too were swept aside by the Wallaby pack, and the backs cleaned up with another four tries. Jones could now afford to be modest. Asked how he felt about his achievement, he refused to crow and settled for a quaint Australian proverb, 'Today a rooster – tomorrow a feather duster: you know how it is.'

But the Australian achievement was immense. They proved that the art of moving the ball quickly was not dead and that the secret of success was to have, first and foremost, fifteen skilful players on the field who all wanted to run and handle. They demonstrated that the British power game would never succeed against a side that could win its own ball and then run at the opposition with support from a mobile pack. They proved that big men can also be athletes.

The Argentine immigrant Enrique Rodriguez and the seventeen-stone hooker, Tom Lawton, proved themselves more than equal to their British opponents as scrummagers, as well as contributing fully in the loose. Steve Cutler scarcely lost a ball in the middle of the line-out and also made a number of telling runs in open play, while Simon Poidevin never stopped running for the whole two months they were in Britain.

In the backs, they had a genius in Mark Ella. He created his own bit of history by scoring a try in each of the internationals, and showed such perception and sleight of hand that he set up scores of opportunities for his captain Andrew Slack and another outside-half who played centre in the Test team, Michael Lynagh. With Brendan Moon on one wing and David Campese on the other, and with fullback Roger Gould joining the line at every opportunity, they were a formidable strike force.

It was the Australians' attitude to the game that will remain in the memory longest. Despite more than their fair share of wet weather, they were still determined to run the ball at every opportunity, and such was their level of skill that they were able to do so successfully even in the worst conditions.

British rugby was deservedly relegated to the second division; a sterile approach after the victories of the Lions in the early Seventies had led to an over concentration on set pieces. If British teams could not control the pace of the game by exerting a vice-like grip on the scrums and line-outs, they had nothing else to offer. Only after a comprehensive beating by a country which had hitherto been below Britain on the rugby ladder, did coaches and players alike begin to reassess their game.

Mark Ella looks for support under pressure from England's Mike Slemen and Paul Dodge. A feature of the Australians' play throughout the tour was their excellent handling and ability to keep the ball on the move.

No 8 Steve Tuynman storms upfield to pave the way for David Campese's second try of the match against Scotland. The Wallabies' overwhelming victory by 37–12 gave them their first-ever 'Grand Slam' against the Home Countries.

Peter Grigg and Michael Lynagh congratulate Mark Ella after his intercept try against Wales.

Second-row man Steve Williams feeds Nick Farr-Jones in the match against Ireland. Fellow forwards Steve Cutler and Enrique Rodriguez are in close support.

Fullback Roger Gould kicks high and handsomely in the match against London Division.

A classic hand-off by Brendan Moon to keep the England international winger Simon Smith at bay in the London Division game.

Left *With a series of outstanding performances on the tour, Steve Cutler firmly established himself as a second-row player of world class.*

The Wallabies' captain Andy Slack moves the ball on before Welsh international Mark Ring can intervene (v Cardiff).

Below *Simon Poidevin, who has exceptional speed for a forward, leaves Underwood, Milne and Gareth Davies behind as he heads for the line. Poidevin contributed two tries to Australia's victory over the Barbarians by 37–30 in the last match of the tour.*

Over *The unthinkable happens at Cardiff as Australia scores a pushover try against Wales. The scorer, buried under the collapsed scrum, is Steve Tuynman.*

KINGS AND PRINCES

Barry John will be mortified reading this. In fact, mentioning him in the first line is the only thing that may persuade him that he should read on. He believes that all forwards are basically illiterate, but even accepting that some will be unwise enough to put pen to paper, he could never credit that a forward would be foolish enough to try to write about things which are beyond his comprehension – like half-backs, the royalty of the rugby field. To him the outside-halves are the kings, and the scrum-halves at least princes.

If he had his way, forwards would carry on their business outside the touchlines, from where the ball would be delivered to the backs who would then play the important part of the game. I can vouch for all this because I played alongside Barry for just about the whole of his international career, and he very soon took the opportunity to put me in my place. My crime was to ask which way the next move was going to develop once we had won the ball.

'Listen, JT,' he said, in a tone reserved for those who belong below stairs. 'Just get us the ball and then stay out of the way, there's a good chap.' He could ooze condescension when he chose. 'You'll only mess up the whole move if you try to join in.' And with that I was dismissed.

It was only later that I realised the real reason for such treatment. He had no clue as to what would happen either, but then that was really the key to why he was the King of Kings.

Scrum-halves are a different breed. They are still in the superstar mould, but by virtue of their role in the game they are a much earthier breed. They must have something of the terrier in them, and unlike their partners, must be prepared to get their hands dirty. If things get tough, they will even get their shorts dirty. Working so closely with the forwards you might expect them to feel some sort of bond, but when the crunch comes they always show their true colours and line up with the piano players rather than the donkeys – John Dawes' definitive perception of the difference between backs and forwards.

We always believed that Gareth Edwards was a good chum; he got muckier than most, and in his younger days even did some tackling. But he lost his honorary forward status forever in 1974 after an incident in practice on the sands at Aberavon. Terry Cobner of Pontypool and Trevor Evans from Swansea were the two flank forwards in the Welsh team, and at last (Barry John had retired) the backs were persuaded

that it was a good idea to let the forwards know which way to run when the scrum broke up.

A simple code, to be relayed by the scrum-half, was devised. Any word beginning with 'P' (for Pontypool) and the forwards broke to Cobner's side; any word beginning with 'S' and they followed Evans. At the first practice Edwards shouted 'PSYCHOLOGY', the forwards took off in both directions and another good scheme bit the dust.

There was one scrum-half who was the exception. Even though he is now a professional, he is still an honorary forward for any member of any pack that played with him. Terry Holmes, Edwards' successor, was such a grafter that he was a genuine ninth forward. He would have made a fine flanker had he wished to play in that position, and at 6ft 1in would certainly not have been the smallest man to play international rugby there. Unfortunately, the great Welsh era was stuttering to a stop by the time he came on the scene and he never played international rugby with a really good supply of ball, or a set of backs that could make the most of what they did receive. As a result, he had to take far too much on his own shoulders, often quite literally, and at times he was a total one-man band.

Had Holmes been part of a more balanced team, I believe he would have developed in a completely different way and been even more effective. Nevertheless, his success was phenomenal; he always posed a threat and managed to score tries even when the opposition knew that if they could stop him they had effectively snuffed out Wales' only attacking option.

Edwards and Holmes allowed only a handful of other Welsh scrum-halves international representation in the years 1967–85. Edwards' record was quite incredible. While winning fifty-three caps between 1967 and 1978 he never missed a major international, though he twice left the field injured, giving 'Chico' Hopkins and Clive Shell their only caps, as replacements.

England, judging by their record over the same period, might have fared better had they been able to settle on their half-backs and allow them to build a partnership. While Edwards ruled in Wales, England called up twelve different scrum-halves – an average of more than one a season. And to make matters worse, they kept dropping and reinstating players like Jacko Page, the excellent Jan Webster and Steve Smith, so that there were twenty-two changes in all. Indeed

England should perhaps have taken more notice of what was going on around them. All the successful countries over the last twenty years have either had experience at half-back or have introduced new talent which they have stuck with until it has had time to find its feet.

New Zealand, the most consistent country of all over the period, have relied principally on just three scrum-halves. Chris Laidlaw was the pivot man when they ruled supreme in the late Sixties, but from 1967 he was understudied by the terrier-like Sid Going. Going then continued until 1977, with Dave Loveridge taking over as first choice for the next six years.

Dawie de Villiers, captain of South Africa at the time of their last tour of the British Isles, is amongst the top ten most-capped players of all time in that country. And, more recently, Jérôme Gallion of France has been one of the most influential figures in his national team. He has only won twenty-three caps since 1978, but would have been up with their leading players had he not spent 1981–2 in the wilderness. There was what is euphemistically called a clash of personality between him and the assistant coach. In Gallic fashion there could be no compromise, so Gallion sat on the sidelines and France suffered until the coach was replaced. Then Gallion missed the whole of the 1986 Five Nations Championship through injury.

Scotland also realise the value of experience. Roy Laidlaw has been under pressure for his place on several occasions, but they have resisted change in favour of continuity; the reward was a big contribution from the thirty-two-year-old as Scotland bounced back from the 'wooden spoon' in 1985 to grab a share of the Championship the following year. During the season Laidlaw set a new world record with John Rutherford for the number of times a pair of half-backs have played together in internationals. By the end of the year, they had lined up together thirty times.

Outside-halves generally do not have the staying power of their partners. There seems to be something in the make-up of the real play-makers in any team that causes most of them to give up early.

Barry John was just twenty-seven, and absolutely in his prime, when he decided that there was nothing more to prove (Cliff Morgan's retirement had been similarly premature in the late Fifties), but fortunately Wales already had a tested replacement in Phil Bennett. Edwards outlasted the pair of them. The most recent loss was Mark Ella. The brilliant Australian had the two great Welshmen roaring approval as he scored a try in each of the four Tests in the Wallabies' first-ever Grand Slam over the Home Countries – then, inexplicably, at the age of twenty-six, he decided to bow out.

Irishmen sometimes feel aggrieved that Wales has become so famous for its fly-half factory. They would argue that they have an equally good production line themselves. The legendary Jackie Kyle has been followed by Mike Gibson – many people forget that he began as an outside-half and won twenty-five caps in that position before moving to centre – the barrel-like Barry McGann, Tony Ward and Ollie Campbell. Ward goes on forever, despite the snubs of the selectors in recent years, but Campbell's was another career halted in full flow, this time by injury and illness.

Outside Britain the mercurial, running outside-half is very much the exception. In France, they tend to go for kickers. Jean-Pierre Romeu, Jean-Pierre Lescarboura and Guy Laporte are first required to slot the goals and clear their lines, then they are drilled to move the ball quickly so that the other backs can attack. Bob Burgess is the great exception amongst New Zealand first five-eighths in recent times, while Naas Botha almost kicked the South African game to a standstill.

But whatever the interpretation of the role of the half-backs, one thing is certain. Without a strong combination no team can be successful. They really are the pivots around which the team functions once it has possession.

Finally, I still refuse to try and settle the argument about who was the better player, Barry John or Phil Bennett. They were both brilliant – but it would not be proper for a mere forward to pass judgement.

For twelve years Gareth Edwards was the pivotal figure in a brilliantly successful Wales side, making a record fifty-three consecutive appearances. He had all the attributes of a great scrum-half, plus explosive strength and power and an insatiable appetite for tries.

Above *Edwards on his way to a try, pursued by Scottish winger Billy Steele, at Cardiff in 1976.*

A textbook pass from the base of the scrum against England at Twickenham in 1974.

Gareth Edwards was never more dangerous than when in sight of the line. Here he plunges past Tony Neary and Charlie Hannaford to touch down – only to have the try disallowed because of an infringement. Wales v England, 1971.

Edwards is first to the ball when he and Welsh flanker John Taylor catch Ireland's Mike Hipwell in possession at Cardiff in 1971.

Roy Laidlaw clears from a pool of water on the rain-soaked pitch at Dunedin during the 3rd Test in 1983. Towering above him is All Black lock Gary Whetton.

Left *Steve Smith, who was in and out of the England side over a period of ten years yet still managed to win a record number of caps for a scrum-half, in action against France in 1982. Watching him get his kick away are Manuel Carpentier and Steve Bainbridge.*

Dawie de Villiers was South Africa's scrum-half during most of the Sixties. He has twenty-five caps to his name, all but three of them as captain – both records for his country.

With Welsh forwards Delme Thomas and Mervyn Davies bearing down on him, scrum-half Roger Young sets up another Irish move. Cardiff, 1971.

The magnificent Australian scrum-half Ken Catchpole, whose productive partnership with Phil Hawthorne was a key factor for the Wallabies in the Sixties, in action against Southern Counties on the 1966–67 tour.

Terry Holmes had the difficult job of taking over from Gareth Edwards in the Welsh side. Despite being somewhat injury-prone, he soon established himself as the finest British scrum-half of his generation. On the world scene his greatest rival was probably Dave Loveridge, seen here in action against him in 1978.

John Hipwell succeeded Ken Catchpole as Australia's No 1 scrum-half and continued to play for his country for the next fourteen years, acquiring a record thirty-four caps. Here, playing in his last Test for Australia, against England in 1982, he takes possession of the ball from a loose maul.

For more than two decades New Zealand has principally relied on just three scrum-halves: Chris Laidlaw, Sid Going and Dave Loveridge.

Left The gritty, pugnacious Sid Going launches into a pass against Wales at Cardiff in 1974, and below makes a penetrating run in loose play during the 2nd Test against the Lions in 1977.

Right Dave Loveridge looks to distribute the ball before being tackled by Roy Laidlaw in the 3rd Test against the Lions in 1983.

Chris Laidlaw, who was an Oxford Blue as well as an All Black, playing for the University against Richmond in 1968.

Being tackled by Gareth Edwards proves a hair-raising experience for Scotland's Doug Morgan at Cardiff in 1976.

French scrum-half Jérôme Gallion makes off with the ball at Parc des Princes in the match against England in 1979.

Right With his flowing mane and willingness to run with the ball whenever he could, fly-half Bob Burgess was one of the more distinctive members of Ian Kirkpatrick's 1972–73 All Blacks.

Left The one and only Barry John – 'King John' the fans dubbed him – whose great partnership with Gareth Edwards is part of rugby history, shows characteristic poise and perfect balance as he attempts a drop goal against England in 1971.

Phil Bennett, who formed a second distinguished partnership with Gareth Edwards, was never far from the action. Right He comes to the rescue of the fallen J. P. R. Williams to clear his lines, under pressure from Scotland's Billy Steele, at Cardiff in 1974. Below A tactical kick ahead against Waikato on the 1977 Lions tour.

The illustrious Richard Sharp, England star of the Sixties, playing for Cornwall against Surrey in the County Championship Semi-Final, 1967.

Fly-half John Rutherford goes over the top to score a try in Scotland's runaway 33-6 victory against England in 1986.

Opposite Twickenham: a spectacular view of the game's headquarters as seen from the newly-erected South Stand.

Less familiar, the high-rise skyline at the Pan-Am International Rugby Tournament in Honolulu.

Patrick Estève of France breaks one of the game's cardinal rules against England in 1985. Heading for the posts after having crossed the line, he fails to touch down in time and is caught by Richard Harding. Winger Rory Underwood is alongside.

Top right *Bill Beaumont and Nigel Horton combine to beat Geoff Wheel and Allan Martin in the line-out. England v Wales, 1978.*

Bottom right *Scrum-half Terry Holmes launches another Welsh attack against New Zealand in 1978, with Derek Quinnell in close support.*

Mark Ella demonstrates the Australians' innovative approach to back-play with a subtle reverse pass to Roger Gould, which throws the English defence and almost results in a try. Twickenham, 1984.

A familiar sight in 1984: Mark Ella heading for the line.

Opposite *Fiji's Dominiko Manaseitava about to score a try against Western Samoa in the 1984 Hong Kong Sevens.*

Kevin Greene gets the ball away in the nick of time as his opposite number Brynmor Williams bears down on him. Waikato v British Lions, 1977.

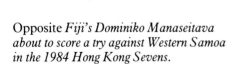

Three exceptional Irish fly-halves of recent years: Tony Ward left, Barry McGann below left and the remarkable Ollie Cambell, who holds all but one of the point-scoring records for his country – and that one he shares with Tony Ward.

Paul McLean, who had a long career kicking for Australia, having another shot at goal against the Midlands on the 1981–82 tour. He also played several Tests at fullback.

South Africa's most capped fly-half, Piet Visagie, aims for the posts at Newport on the Springboks' last tour of the British Isles in 1969.

THE LIONS IN SOUTH AFRICA

For rugby players who can convince themselves that playing in South Africa has nothing to do with supporting apartheid, or who do not care in any case, a tour to the Republic is just about perfect.

In contrast to New Zealand, they can rely upon the sun shining most of the time; swimming and sunbathing therefore become options during time off, and there are even some nice easy fixtures thrown in midweek on a long tour which do not have to be taken too seriously. A visit to the Kruger Park halfway through has always been an added attraction for the British Lions.

Victory in a Test series would make life just about perfect, but that had proved beyond any Lions' team this century when the 1974 side set off under the leadership of Willie John McBride, who was making a record fifth Lions tour and visiting South Africa for the third time. They knew they had the best chance they would ever get to win a series. Included in the party was a hard core of players who had experienced victory with the 1971 Lions in New Zealand. McBride, Ian McLauchlan (the Mighty Mouse), Gordon Brown and Mervyn Davies had all played in the Tests on that tour and Fergus Slattery had matured into a fine player, so there was the nucleus for a powerful Test pack. Behind the scrum, Gareth Edwards and J. P. R. Williams were at the height of their powers.

To complete the scrum, they introduced the abrasive Welsh hooker Bobby Windsor and the giant England prop Fran Cotton to the front row, and moved Roger Uttley to blind-side wing forward. The front row looked extremely odd with McLauchlan the smallest at 5ft 8in on the left, Windsor at 5ft 10in in the middle, and then Cotton at 6ft 2in on the tight head. The Springbok selections were all much bigger, but just as he had done in New Zealand, the 'Mighty Mouse' burrowed under his opponent and, despite his lack of weight, none of them could move him.

Phil Bennett took over the outside-half role and revelled in the firm conditions. It was on this tour that he found the confidence to play in internationals as he did for Llanelli or the Barbarians. For Wales up to this point he had been over-cautious. The Irishman Dick Milliken was paired with Ian McGeechan from Scotland in the centre, with the Welsh sprinter J. J. Williams on one wing. Billie Steele played in the first two Tests on the right wing, but was then replaced by the second fullback, Andy Irvine. Although he could not match the physical presence of J. P. R. Williams, he was too good a footballer to leave out.

After winning the first Test through the boot of Bennett and an Edwards dropped goal, they ran in ten tries in the next three matches and set a host of scoring records for teams visiting South Africa. The second Test victory by 28-9 was the biggest defeat suffered by the Springboks in an international match, and was followed by the slightly narrower margin of 26-9 in the third Test.

The forwards really dominated the series and it was no coincidence that Gordon Brown, the big Scottish lock, scored two tries – no doubt yelling, 'You beauty,' as he plunged over. We never saw the best of 'Stookie Broon' in Britain; he needed the full-time devotion to training that a Lions tour allowed him to get really fit. Then he was a mighty forward and woe betide anybody who thought they could take liberties just because he had a baby face. He could be as mean as Willie John.

McBride's men returned as the most successful Lions ever, with only one blemish on their record – a draw in the final Test. Having won the series, most teams would have been content and might even have eased off; but not this team. They were furious that the referee disallowed a try which they were certain Fergus Slattery had scored in the closing minutes of the game.

The 1980 Lions had high hopes of emulating the 1974 team. They were led by Billy Beaumont, fresh from leading England to their first Grand Slam since 1957, and looked to have a powerful squad. However, it was not to be.

The one thing wrong with South Africa is the hard grounds. There are often bone-hard cricket wickets in the middle of some of the provincial pitches and if you fall on them at the wrong angle, your tour is over. The 1980 side suffered more than any other team before. With Mike Slemen returning home because of the death of his father and Fran Cotton believing for a while that he had had a heart attack, the Lions had to call on a record eight replacements. Even so, they ran the Springboks close in the first three Tests, losing 26-22, 26-19 and 12-10, before showing great character by winning the final match 17-13.

Clive Woodward, chased by Springbok fly-half Naas Botha, has Ray Gravell (left) and Bruce Hay in support, 2nd Test, 1980.

Tom David, Gordon Brown and Mervyn Davies celebrate the Lions' victory in the 3rd Test at Port Elizabeth in 1974.

Hands off, says Bruce Hay, on an attacking run against Northern Transvaal in 1980.

Lions' back-row man Roger Uttley is caught in possession against Eastern Transvaal, 1974.

Above right *Springbok scrum-half Divan Serfontein clears under pressure from Peter Wheeler, the Lions' hooker, in the 3rd Test, 1980.*

Winger Gerrie Germishuys wrong-foots his opposite number John Carleton and links up with support players Rob Louw, Martiens le Roux, and Willie du Plessis (right). 2nd Test, 1980.

Left *Bill Beaumont riding high on the shoulders of Springbok lock Moaner van Heerden; and (below) bottom of the pile, with Springboks Prentis, Moolman and le Roux, and team-mate Maurice Colclough.*

The celebrations go on after the Lions' victory in the 3rd Test in 1974, (l to r) Ian McLauchlan, Stewart McKinney, Andy Irvine, captain Willie John McBride and, about to be garrotted, coach Syd Millar.

Below *Gordon Brown dives past D. Sonnekus to score a try – to the obvious delight of Bobby Windsor and Fran Cotton. 3rd Test, 1974.*

Over *The massed ranks of South African fans at Ellis Park, Johannesburg, in 1974, accommodated in a temporary stand supported only by scaffolding.*

1

2

3

4

Welsh winger J. J. Williams runs round to the posts, pursued by an impressively agile Hannes Marais, the Springbok captain and prop forward, to score a splendid try in the 3rd Test. Williams notched two tries in the match, which the Lions won convincingly 26-9 to take the series. Not surprisingly, perhaps, some of the home crowd seem to be as jubilant as Williams himself.

Flanker Rob Louw, tackled by Andy Irvine, looks for support from Willie du Plessis. 2nd Test, 1980.

Above right *A typical charge by Andy Ripley and Roger Uttley in the match against The Leopards in 1974 – the first time that a Lions' side had played against a non-white team in South Africa.*

Fergus Slattery moves alongside as Mervyn Davies is caught by Springbok forward Kritzinger in the 4th Test in 1974. The match was drawn, depriving the Lions of a clean sweep.

SNAP
SELECTION 3

Erika Roe being escorted off the field by two over-dressed policemen after her topless appearance at halftime during the England v Australia match at Twickenham in 1982.

Above right All Black forwards get down to some intensive scrummaging practice under the eye of coach Bob Duff, himself a former New Zealand lock, at Peebles in Scotland in 1972.

Far right Terry Cobner caught with his pants down.

The best-looking scrum down in the history of the game. Actresses v Models at London Irish, 1974.

BACK ROW

I never intended to be a back-row forward. Gerald Davies converted me, not by wise counsel or because he thought he had spotted some special talent for the position, but by running around me far too easily on several occasions when we were both playing in the centre at Loughborough as students. Having made the move out of expediency, it was gratifying to learn that many of the other players who ended up there were also rejects from other positions.

Jean-Pierre Rives was one such player, and summed up his own talents very honestly: 'I am not very big, not very fast, not very strong but I am not small, slow or weak either, so thank God for a position where I can make the most of my strengths.' Playing at wing forward certainly allows you to do that. It is a position which enables you to make the most of what you have and adapt your game accordingly, compensating for lack of physique with speed or using strength to cover lack of mobility.

There is an answer to almost everything except, as once happened to me, another flanker who marches up to you in the clubhouse and says, 'Listen, I'm taller than you, heavier than you and faster than you, so how come you are playing for Wales and not me?'

Number 8s are totally different. There have been some good small ones like Tommy Bedford and Alex Wyllie, but the great ones are all very tall, rangy and utterly reliable, which is why they often make good captains as well. Brian Lochore, Morne du Plessis, Mervyn Davies and Benoit Dauga are all peas from the same pod, with Walter Spanghero a slightly smaller, chunkier version. Where open-side flankers indulge themselves in explosive displays of temper, they remain calm and pick up the pieces; they are reassuring to have around, even if most of them cannot pass.

Around 1970 Wales produced a coaching directive that advocated a new approach towards back-row play. Central to the theme was the selection of big men on the flanks as well as at Number 8. It came as a bitter blow to me and the other wing forward in the Welsh team, Dai Morris. I never made it to six feet and Dai was only an inch or so taller. Whatever the programme notes said, neither of us topped fourteen stones soaking wet. We both thought we had played our last international, but fortunately there was a shortage of mobile giants in Wales and the selectors had different ideas to the coaching staff, so we survived.

At that time New Zealand had just defeated Wales heavily in two internationals and the feeling was that we had to have men with physiques to match those of the likes of Kel Tremain and Ian Kirkpatrick. Neither would have been out of place in the second row, but could run as well. Kirkpatrick, in particular, was fast enough to run half the length of the field to score, given the chance, as he showed in the second Test against the 1971 Lions.

But the small flanker still survives. Mike Rafter was perhaps the most remarkable. He was the shortest of us all but still played seventeen times for England, nearly always operating on the blind side.

Back rows are all about balance. As Mervyn Davies never tired of telling me, he was the only reason that Wales could afford the luxury of two smallish men. He was such a dominant force in the line-out that he would often steal ball intended for the middle-line jumper as well as grabbing all his own. The same applied with France when they had Jean-Pierre Bastiat playing at Number 8. Jean-Pierre Rives and Jean-Claude Skréla were ideal foragers to go with him, but as soon as Bastiat retired Skréla lost his place, even though many people believe he played some of his best rugby after 1978.

Another factor is the style of play generally associated with particular countries. New Zealand have always been the masters of driving forward-play and have therefore produced men who are good at that. Alan Sutherland and 'Cowboy' Mark Shaw came out of the same mould as Tremain and Kirkpatrick. They were a fearsome sight coming at you, but were not quite so good if you could win enough ball to spread it wide and make them chase threequarters. There Graham Mourie was the exception to the archetypal All Black flanker. He was much more in the European style because by this time New Zealand were playing a much more expansive game. Mourie was, for me, the best, most complete player of all. He had the pace and perception of Fergus Slattery or Tony Neary in support of his backs, and was equally at home driving in concert with his big forwards. He was also a superb tackler, and nobody has ever covered more ground in the course of a game.

In Britain, we have often had to manufacture big flankers by borrowing them from other positions. The 1971 Lions decided that one big man was essential in support of Mervyn Davies, so Peter Dixon and Derek Quinnell were brought in to the line-up. In 1974 Roger Uttley proved a more than useful stopgap, but afterwards they all reverted to No 8 or second row.

The same problem exists today. While the rest of the world are moving towards bigger and more powerful back rows – France fielded three men all over 6ft 3in tall in the 1986 Championship – the four home countries just cannot find them. It is good to see that there is still a place for the little men, but for them to operate effectively, we need a few more like John Jeffrey and Jon Hall.

The flamboyant Jean-Pierre Rives, for years a tour de force on the side of the French scrum. Here he receives massive protection from the 6ft 7in No 8 Jean-Pierre Bastiat, who single-handedly restrains Fran Cotton and Bill Beaumont. Robin Cowling is on the right of the picture. England v France, 1977.

An object lesson in defensive covering from the ubiquitous Graham Mourie as he hauls down Welsh flyer J. J. Williams just short of the goal-line. Cardiff, 1978.

Budge Rogers, one of the star names of the Sixties, playing for East Midlands against the Barbarians in 1968.

Right *The dashing figure of Fergus Slattery, whose international career spanned thirteen years and sixty-one caps – a record for an Irish flanker.*

Welsh flanker Dai Morris feeds the ball to Gareth Edwards, watched by Denzil Williams and Delme Thomas. Wales v England, 1971.

Textbook protection for Alan Sutherland,
the All Black No 8, is given by Alex
Wyllie left and Ian Eliason, in the match
against Cambridge University in 1972.

Above right *The Adonis-like figure of
Andy Ripley, playing in England's back
row against Australia at Brisbane in
1975. On the right is Dave Rollit.*

Right *No 8 Benoit Dauga, considered by
many to be the greatest French forward of
all time. Behind him is a formidable line-
up of French forward power: the two
Spanghero brothers left and Christian
Carrère and Michel Yachvili right.*

Welsh No 8 Mervyn Davies pounces on
the loose ball following a Gerald Davies
tackle. Wales v France, 1976.

Two try-scoring No 8s:
Above *Derek Quinnell hands off Mike Biggar on his way to a try for Wales against Scotland in 1978.*

Right *Scotland's Peter Brown joyfully plunges over the line against England in 1971.*

Left *The great New Zealand forward Ian Kirkpatrick powers his way upfield in the 4th Test against the Lions in 1977.*

Welsh flanker John Taylor breaks across field as scrum-half Jan Webster sets up an England attack in the 1972 game.

Right *The more famous of the two Spangheros, Walter, the brilliant French No 8, shares possession of the ball with brother Claude* left.

Simon Poidevin, the Australian flanker, who has established himself in the front rank of modern back-row players, in action for the Overseas Unions against the Five Nations at Twickenham in 1986.

RUGBY JAPANESE STYLE

The Japanese made many friends on their first tour of the UK in 1973. They impressed with their speed and general open style of play, but were outmatched in the forwards, winning only one of their seven games. When they returned ten years later, the Japanese came very close to beating Wales, with a final scoreline of 29-24. Left *fullback Naohisa Tanifuji scythes through the Welsh defence.*

Hooker Mitsuo Atokawa feeds the ball to his scrum-half in the game against the England Under 23 side in 1973. Despite a good performance, the visitors lost 19-10.

Right *Captain Okira Yokoi comes agonisingly close to scoring a try against the mighty Welsh in 1973. Having evaded Gerald Davies, he heads for the corner, only to be pushed into touch via the flag by a diving tackle from Clive Shell. Wales won 62-14.*

TRIES SCORED AND TRIES MISSED

Mike Slemen and Bob Hesford can do nothing to stop Scotland's Jim Calder scoring in the Calcutta Cup match of 1981.

This time it is Ireland's Trevor Ringland and Michael Kiernan who are left standing by Mike Slemen at Twickenham in 1982.

Left An evergreen Kevin Flynn, a month away from his thirty-third birthday, crosses the line against England in 1972. About to join in the celebrations, over the fallen Alan Old, is Ireland's Mike Gibson.

Jérôme Gallion is helped over the line by Philippe Dintrans against England in 1984.

Mervyn Davies shrugs off Andy Leslie and Kent Lambert to score a last-minute equaliser for the Barbarians against the 1974 All Blacks.

Opposite Ray McLoughlin, playing for Ireland against Wales in 1975, beats Mervyn Davies (on the ground), Graham Price and Terry Cobner to a loose ball.

On their return from New Zealand the 1977 British Lions played and beat the Barbarians at Twickenham. Here J. P. R. Williams is determinedly tackled by Peter Squires, but still keeps possession of the ball. Also on hand are Steve Fenwick and Ian McGeechan.

Left *Polar conditions in the '81 Varsity Match and mud-baths all round for the Australian and Tongan teams in the 1983 Hong Kong Sevens.*

Above *Bobby Windsor and Mike Knill screen the ball as Michel Palmié of France bursts through the middle. Knill, who came on as a replacement in the 1976 game, was making his one and only appearance for Wales.*

Going, going, gone – Doug Morgan arrives too late to prevent the redoubtable Sid Going from feeding the ball out to his backs. NZ Maoris v British Lions, 1977.

Opposite *French centre Didier Codorniou races away from Ollie Campbell and Dave Irwin in the match against Ireland in 1984.*

Gareth Edwards scoring the last of his record twenty tries for Wales, against Scotland in 1978.

A contrast in styles: Right *John Bevan, all power and aggression, crashes past Pierre Villepreux to score against France in 1972.* Below *French centre Jean-Pierre Lux touches down with Gallic finesse and flair at Cardiff in 1974.*

Scotland's try against South Africa at Murrayfield in 1969. It was the only try of the match, which Scotland won 6-3.

Above *Scottish centre John Frame breaks through the South African defence, with fullback Ian Smith coming into the line alongside him. Stepping over the fallen Springbok Piet Greyling is Ian Robertson, with Jan Ellis on his left.*

Centre *Smith continues the move with Tommy Bedford and Syd Nomis racing across to intercept.*

Below *Bedford's tackle is too late to prevent Smith scoring. Alastair Biggar raises his arms in triumph.*

Above left *The expression on Paul Simpson's face says it all as he crosses the line for Northern Division against the 1983 All Blacks. Murray Mexted, on the ground, is less thrilled.*

Left *A tackle neither will ever forget. J. P. R. Williams slams French winger Jean-François Gourdon into touch inches from the line. Wales v France, 1976.*

Above left *A happy hooker. Peter Wheeler collects his only try of the tour for the 1977 Lions against the Combined side at Timaru.*

The genius of Gerald Davies in attack and defence. Opposite The Welsh winger takes Arthur McMaster with him as he scores against Ireland in 1975. Above A flying Gerald Davies catches French winger Sillières just short of the line and, in a smother tackle, pins his arms and rolls him into touch through the corner flag, preventing the Frenchman from grounding or releasing the ball.

SNAP SELECTION 4

The golden boy of French rugby, Jean-Pierre Rives.

Below *The NSW Country XV adopt their famous 'up the jumper' ploy to confuse Roger Uttley and the rest of the England team on the 1975 tour of Australia.*

Above right *The final whistle goes and N.W. Counties becomes the first English provincial side ever to beat New Zealand, 1972.*

Below right *A sudden hailstorm almost obliterates the players in the John Player Cup Semi-Final between Bristol and Harlequins in 1984.*

SECOND ROW

Second rows are not made, they are born. If you were holding auditions you would start by telling anybody under 6ft 4in and 225lb that they need not bother to apply, and the same would go for anybody who was not mean, awkward and quick to take offence. The born second row asks no favours and gives no favours. In his world the nice guys always come second. They bristle with aggression. To give an inch is to surrender.

It is the one position in rugby where there is absolutely no substitute for size. The priorities are to lock the scrums and win the line-outs; the rest is a bonus. Bill McLaren, for many people the voice of rugby, likes to describe them as being in the 'boiler-house'. It is an apt description. Without boilers you have no power; without effective second rows you have no primary possession, and therefore no hope.

Colin Meads was probably the greatest lock of his time. Fifteen years after retiring he is still an awesome figure, and it is not just his size, although he is as lean and massive as ever. He just exudes a quiet menace that tells the world he was a second row and was not to be messed with. Brian Thomas, Willie John McBride, Nigel Horton, Alain Estève and Elie Cester gave off the same vibrations.

The line-out used to be the battleground where supremacy was decided. When there was no gap between the lines and no gap between the players it was a free for all, and it was very seldom the man who could jump highest who won the ball. Meads often secured possession by standing firm while mayhem was going on all around him. He was protected just like the quarterback in American Football and if there was any interference he would be quite ruthless in dealing with it, as Jeff Young testified through his wired teeth the day after the first Test in 1969.

If you did have a high jumper, he had to be protected. At six foot three Delme Thomas only just made the grade, but he had such an exceptional leap he could outjump any opponent; but he would have been totally ineffective had it not been for Denzil Williams who acted as his minder, clearing a space for him to jump and sometimes adding in a sly lift.

Now with the law requiring a gap between players and between the lines, the line-out is a much more orderly affair; so the emphasis has shifted. Longer, leaner men can be effective, as Steve Cutler of Australia and Steve Bainbridge and Wade Dooley of England have proved. The general trend is also towards more mobility. The French have always produced running tight forwards, but in the rest of the rugby world they have been the exception rather than the rule. Frik du Preez of South Africa and the young Meads spring to mind as outstanding in the loose, but in the home countries any tight forward who was too conspicuous was likely to be accused of being a 'seagull' and not doing his fair share in the set pieces. Billy Beaumont had his moments and Gordon Brown proved he could do both when he was fit, which was only on Lions tours, but the majority settled for being solid rather than spectacular.

The French have never had any such inhibitions. In the late Sixties and early Seventies, they used to swap Walter Spanghero and Benoit Dauga around between the second row and Number 8 almost match by match. Rumour had it that they both wanted the Number 8 spot, so the one who was more sluggish in practice had to move up. Spanghero was obviously marginally sharper. He won twenty-six caps in the back row and sixteen at lock, while over an almost identical period Dauga won twenty-nine at lock and twenty-one at Number 8.

In the four home countries Scotland have taken the lead by converting Iain Paxton, who had won twenty-one caps in the back row, but the other three are still producing old-fashioned forwards. Poor Wales just cannot find players of the right size at the moment. Take away Bob Norster and Richard Moriarty (and they ruled themselves out in 1986 by being sent off) and there is not another player who measures up to the basics. Now they realise how the poor Japanese feel after years of fighting and losing the unequal battle.

Australian Dave Hillhouse rises unaided above the rest of the line to make a clean deflection to scrum-half Rod Hauser at Twickenham in 1976.

Two great rivals, England's Nigel Horton and Ireland's Moss Keane, clash at the line-out. Fran Cotton lends a helping hand.

Left *All Black lock Frank Oliver ready to leap into action against Cardiff on the 1978 tour. Oliver was involved in the controversial line-out decision on the same tour which led to New Zealand's victory against Wales by one point.*

Frik du Preez, who remains South Africa's most-capped lock, was an outstanding player in the loose. He also appeared for the Springboks on seven occasions as a flanker. Seen here in action against Newport in 1969.

Welshman Geoff Wheel had immense upper-body strength, which made him a formidable opponent, particularly in a maul. In the picture, team-mate Bobby Windsor moves in to collect the ball from him.

Leading from the front. Captain Bill Beaumont, with Roger Uttley in support, takes on Jim Renwick in England's 'Grand Slam' match against Scotland in 1980.

Peter Whiting, one of New Zealand's great line-out specialists, demonstrates his skill against the Barbarians in 1974.

Above right *Not an everyday occurrence for a second-row man. England's Chris Ralston scoring against Ireland in 1972.*

Right *A classic two-handed take by an airborne Richard Moriarty for Wales against Australia in 1981.*

Left Welshman Bob Norster wins line-out possession against England in 1983. Team-mate Jeff Squire is alongside.

Below left All Black centre Ian Hurst has the unenviable task of stopping the massive Frenchman Alain Estève, with fellow lock Elie Cester coming up fast behind. Paris, 1973.

One of the true giants of the game: All Black Colin Meads playing for the President's Overseas XV against England in 1971.

Below Former England second-row man Peter Larter (headband) playing for the Barbarians v East Midlands in 1968. Also in the picture, Tommy Bedford far left, Peter Bell centre with Bob Taylor behind him, and scrum-half Nigel Starmer-Smith.

Over Maurice Colclough wins the ball for Nick Youngs, despite the intervention of All Black prop Brian McGrattan. Twickenham, 1983.

Brian Price knocks the ball down from a line-out watched by team-mates Dai Morris and Denzil Williams, and Irish prop Syd Millar right.

Irish lock Donal Lenihan disputes a line-out with Frenchman Jean Condom, while scrum-half Jérôme Gallion awaits the outcome. Paris, 1984.

THE ALL BLACKS ARE COMING

The first New Zealanders, an all Maori team, toured the UK and Ireland in 1888–9. Before 1967 there were then another five major tours, in 1905–6, 1924–5, 1935–6, 1953–4 and 1963–4, plus another visit from the Maoris, with no Tests against the home countries but one in France, in 1926–7. In the last twenty years there have been seven visits to the UK and/or Ireland, plus two separate tours to France. The reason for the sudden increase in tours was partly compensation for the loss of revenue to the Home Unions caused by the absence of South Africa – since the anti-apartheid demonstrations in 1969–70 nobody has thought of bringing a South African national team to Britain – and partly the ease with which one could now travel between the two countries. Even in 1950 the Lions travelled to New Zealand by boat, which added twelve weeks to the length of the tour.

The Home Unions, like all the International Board countries, rely on the income from tours to keep going. They were undoubtedly very grateful for the revenue that these tours produced, but perhaps greedy as well, because the amount of touring the New Zealanders were asked to undertake has had a far-reaching effect on the game.

There has been a great deal said by the Home Unions about the pressure on players. The British season certainly demands more from a top player than that of any other country, but those demands are nothing compared to what was asked of New Zealand players because of international tour commitments between 1975 and 1980. The frequency of those tours led to a climate of player power; they said, quite naturally, that as they were giving up their own careers and earning so much for the Rugby Unions, they should be compensated. At the 1986 International Board Meeting the whole touring schedule for the next fifteen years was rationalised and scaled down, but it may well be too late to turn back the clock, especially as South Africa is now operating outside all the accepted conventions for organising tours.

Even more importantly, the number of visits took away some of the lustre of a tour by the All Blacks. Until 1972 it was the biggest event in the UK rugby calendar. The public would book months in advance to ensure a chance to watch the players from the other side of the world about whom they had heard so much, but had never seen. The players would deem it the chance of a lifetime to line up against the little country from 12,000 miles away, which from a population of just three million consistently produced so many great players.

There was an aura of mystery and excitement that evaporated totally when the New Zealanders were here during three successive winters from 1978 to 1980. The traditional farewell 'Now is the hour for us to say goodbye, soon we'll be sailing far across the sea,' which had been a very emotional occasion after the final game (added to because the Barbarians always included players from all four countries) now became trite and hollow. It was one thing getting carried away when you knew they would probably never play in Britain again, but quite a different matter when the vast majority would be back the following season. Graham Mourie summed it up at the end of the 1979 tour: 'It's the eternal winter,' he said. 'I go home for our season and then just when summer is coming, it's off to another European winter. I think I'll take up golf, at least they follow the sun.' Mourie captained the All Blacks on five European tours for five seasons on the trot, starting in 1977.

The situation came to a head in 1983. In June and July the All Blacks whitewashed the Lions in a four-Test series in New Zealand, then, having been to South Africa on an unofficial visit, the front five forwards decided they could not afford the time to tour England and Scotland in October and November. As a result, New Zealand drew with Scotland and lost to England for only the second time at Twickenham. It was a credit to the determination and all-round strength of earlier sides that New Zealand did so well during the Seventies, when British rugby was at its strongest. In that period they won eleven Tests and drew one, against Ireland in 1972.

There were some advantages in the All Blacks visiting so often. We saw a great deal more of Graham Mourie than we would have otherwise, and were able to watch him blossom into one of the truly great players of the era. We also had a couple of extra curtain calls from one of the great gentlemen of the game, Bryan Williams.

But it was not all roses. The 1978 game against Wales was only won as a result of one of the worst examples of gamesmanship ever seen on a rugby field. Wales were leading 12-10 with about five minutes to go when Andy Haden and Frank Oliver both dived out of a line-out, totally fooling referee Roger Quittenton, and giving Brian McKechnie a match-winning shot at goal. It was the first but by no means the last sensation in Haden's long career.

There was one famous victory, won by the Barbarians at the end of the 1972–3 tour. The try scored by Gareth Edwards, after Phil Bennett had counter-attacked from under his own posts, has probably been replayed on television (in Britain but perhaps not in New Zealand) more than any other try ever scored.

A temporary inconvenience for Grant Batty whilst playing against the Combined Services in 1972.

Above left *The welcoming sight of the New Zealand haka at the start of the match against Cardiff in 1978.*

Left *The All Black forwards in the line-out give scrum-half Mark Donaldson protection in typical fashion against West Wales at Llanelli in 1978.*

A brilliant opportunist try by scrum-half Dave Loveridge against Scotland in 1979. Winning possession of the ball, he makes to pass outside to Eddie Dunn, sending the Scottish defence in that direction. Then, spotting an opening to his left, he cuts inside to score, completely wrong-footing Alan Lawson, Ian Lambie and Colin Deans – who can't believe what has happened.

Below J. P. R. Williams loses the ball as All Black forwards Keith Murdoch, Ian Kirkpatrick and Tane Norton close in for the kill. Wales v NZ, 1972.

All Black captain Stu Wilson congratulates Peter Wheeler, his opposite number, after the Midlands' victory over New Zealand in 1983.

Fly-half Bob Burgess scoring a try against Neath and Aberavon in 1972.

Graham Whiting, Ian Eliason, Andy Haden and Ian Kirkpatrick combine to gain possession against N.W.Counties in 1972.

Left *Almost a New Zealand institution. The elevating Andy Haden, automatic choice at lock for the past decade.*

Sid Going and Alan Sutherland were a deadly combination round the base of the scrum. Seen here in action against Gwent in 1972.

Right *A late tackle by Tom David after Grant Batty had kicked ahead leads to a sharp altercation on the touchline between the two players, neither of whom was famous for turning the other cheek. Barbarians v NZ, 1973.*

Three of the great names of the era, Ian Kirkpatrick, Sid Going and Walter Spanghero, at Parc des Princes in 1973.

All Black No 8 Murray Mexted is a tough proposition for Adrian Alexander in the match against London Division, 1979.

Bottom right *That's all four, says Andy Haden, after New Zealand's 'Grand Slam' victory over Scotland in 1978. Captain Graham Mourie almost agrees.*

Above left *The All Black pack prepares for a scrum down against Swansea in 1980: (front row) Gary Knight, Hika Reid, Rod Ketels; (second row) Graeme Higginson, Andy Haden; (back row) Mark Shaw, Graham Mourie.*

A tenacious Alex Wyllie en route to a try against Cambridge University in 1972.

FRONT ROW

There is a mystique which surrounds front-row forwards which is totally incomprehensible to the outside world, and in that I include the rest of the team. Nobody except a prop or a hooker would tolerate being put into a crusher forty or more times a game. Second rows complain about being sandwiched, but at least all the effort is going in the same direction; if a prop cannot take the strain, he is likely to break in half.

You can spot a prop from a mile off. He usually looks totally unathletic, has no neck, cauliflower ears (but is too thickset to be a boxer), and in later life walks around with bandy legs and suffers from back trouble. Yet front-row forwards tend to keep playing longer than most other players and are always volunteering for extra scrummaging practice. In short, they are a breed apart.

Their reward comes in later life because there is more folklore involving the front row than the rest of the team put together. Their prodigious feats of strength and bravery, on and off the field, are remembered long after they have quit. The background changes, but the stories are essentially the same around the world.

In Wales, the legendary figures were always miners who could cut more coal in a shift than any other two men. They would always work the morning shift on the day of the match and would then emerge from the darkness to sink five pints at lunchtime – just to settle the dust – before destroying the opposition. After the match they would drink until midnight, then return to the coal-face to hew out another ten tons of black gold.

In the rest of the world, they were always farmers. In New Zealand the legend normally involves rescuing sheep from the snow single-handed, carrying them back, one under each arm, until the whole flock is saved. In Zimbabwe, in the days when it was Rhodesia and in rugby terms a part of South Africa, I even met an ex-Springbok who had wrestled with a cattle-thieving lion (the type that has never heard of rugby) before he got round to killing it. In England, just a couple of years back, Colin White, the Gosforth prop, cut off some fingers in a farming accident and calmly drove to hospital on his tractor to have them sewn back again.

Nobody except those involved understands what really goes on up front in a scrum, so there is a tremendous bond between them. Throughout the world you will find opposing props and hookers locked in conversation after a match, just as they were locked in combat during it. Until a few years ago that made no sense either. Ask a simple question like, 'What was the score?' and the answer would usually be something like 1-0 or 3-2. Games which had been badly lost were victories as far as they were concerned because they had taken more heels against the head.

That has changed, but only a little, with the new scrummaging laws, which make the contortions which hookers and tight-heads specialise in illegal. Sadly, in the eyes of the old specialists, the art of heeling against the head has disappeared. Even the phenomenal technique and upper-body strength of a player like Ray McLoughlin, the Irish prop who used to lock his opponents in a vice-like grip and take them so close to the ground that they found it impossible to push against him, has been rendered useless.

So the role of the prop and the hooker has changed. They are far less specialist and are expected to contribute far more in the loose. Hookers like Colin Deans of Scotland, Peter Wheeler of England and Alan Phillips of Wales were picked for their mobility as much as their striking.

But the Pontypool front row perhaps did most to break the mould. They were very much the hard men of the team but, not content with becoming the first club unit to play together for their country in modern times, they broke all the front-row conventions and each scored a try in their first season. It almost caused suspension from the Front Row Union.

Tries usually come only after years of service as a special reward to set the seal on a glorious career. Denzil Williams, the great Welsh prop who held the national record for appearances until overtaken by Graham Price, was determined to score for his country and eventually achieved it against Ireland in 1969. Keith Jarrett was moving up to take a penalty kick at goal and the Irish were trudging back behind their own line, when the big man appeared at Jarrett's shoulder bellowing like a charging elephant. Jarrett quickly tapped the penalty and Williams was over in the corner before the bewildered Irish knew what had happened.

All Black Keith Murdoch's celebrations of the try he scored to beat Wales in 1972 were so excessive that they ended his career. Security guards in Welsh hotels should know what it means for a prop to score and should stay out of the way of a man who has just achieved a life-time ambition. Front-row forwards may spend most of their lives forced to exist like troglodyte masochists, but you only have to look at the sheer joy on Charlie Faulkner's face after *his* try to realise that deep down there is a flying winger dying to get out.

Welsh prop Denzil Williams, with Delme Thomas and Mervyn Davies in support, feeds Gareth Edwards. Willie John McBride attempts to intercept. Wales v Ireland, 1971.

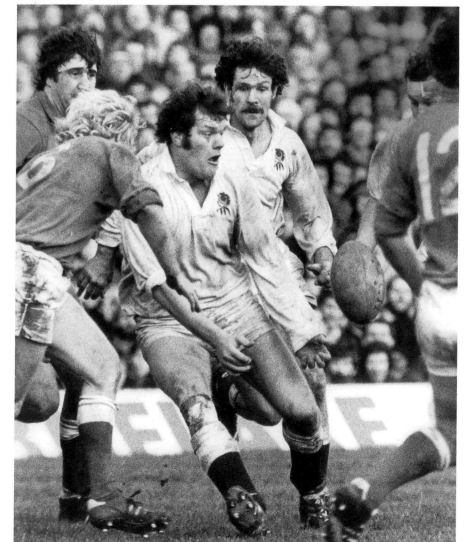

Fran Cotton, who gave England yeoman service over the years, playing against France in 1977 – flanked by Jean-Pierre Rives and Peter Dixon.

Over *Profile of an All Black front row: Gary Knight, Andy Dalton and John Ashworth in the 3rd Test v the Lions in 1983.*

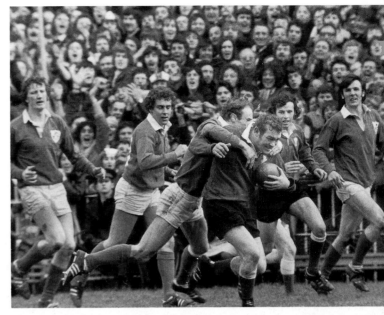

Above left *The famous Pontypool front row of Graham Price, Bobby Windsor and Charlie Faulkner, who followed club and international honours by representing the British Lions, about to get down to it against Bay of Plenty in 1977.*

With just ten yards to go nothing can come between Charlie Faulkner and his try. Even Mike Gibson's determined tackle has little effect on the Welsh prop as he grounds the ball. Winger J. J. Williams, who knows a good try when he sees one, joins in the celebration. Wales v Ireland, 1975.

Left *Clash of the titans. 'Stack' Stevens, later to become an England selector, receiving a crunching tackle from Irish prop Ray McLoughlin in the 1974 game between the two countries. Scrum-half John Moloney leaves them to it.*

Ian McLauchlan – 'The Mighty Mouse' – who captained Scotland more times than anyone else, and whose tremendous scrummaging powers were respected the world over. Here he prepares to do battle once again with New Zealand in 1979.

Right Sandy Carmichael, Ian McLauchlan's partner for so many years, shows exceptional mobility for a prop in catching Welsh winger Gerald Davies in possession. Cardiff, 1976.

Below right Ireland and British Lions' prop Sean Lynch beats Delme Thomas to the ball at Cardiff in 1971. Flanker Denis Hickie stands by.

The great Robert Paparemborde, who has played more times for France than any other prop forward, passes to Jérôme Gallion against England in 1978.

England hooker John Pullin watches as prop Mike Burton feeds the ball back. Burton's arch rival Gérard Cholley tries to find a way through. Paris, 1976.

Peter Wheeler was England's hooker for the best part of ten years, never giving less than a 100 per cent performance. In characteristic style he attempts to charge down a kick by Scotland's Roy Laidlaw. Twickenham, 1983.

SNAP SELECTION 5

Above right *It's sink or swim time for Steve Holdstock, Jim Syddall, Tony Bond and David Cooke during a rest-day regatta in Cleveland on the 1982 England tour of America.*

Gosforth's Steve Gustard and Harry Patrick take a celebratory dip after beating Rosslyn Park in the John Player Cup Final, 1976.

Gordon Brown and Willie John McBride still celebrating the day after their 3rd Test victory against South Africa in 1974.

Jean-Pierre Bastiat braving the elements during a French training session at Windsor in 1977.

Bill Beaumont OBE, 1982.